Classic Brandy

In the same series:

Classic Rum
Julie Arkell

Classic Cocktails
Salvatore Calabrese

Classic Gin
Geraldine Coates

Classic Vodka
Nicholas Faith & Ian Wisniewski

Classic Blended Scotch
Jim Murray

Classic Bourbon, Tennessee and Rye Whiskey
Jim Murray

Classic Irish Whiskey
Jim Murray

Classic Bottled Beers of the World
Roger Protz

Classic Stout and Porter
Roger Protz

Classic Tequila
Ian Wisniewski

CLASSIC BRANDY

NICHOLAS FAITH

First published in 2000 in Great Britain by
Prion Books Limited
Imperial Works, Perren Street
London NW5 3ED

© PRION BOOKS LIMITED
Text copyright © Nicholas Faith 2000
Designed by DW Design

All rights reserved.

No part of this book may be reproduced, stored in a retrieval system, or transmitted in any form or by any means, electronic, mechanical, photocopying, recording or otherwise, without the prior written permission of the publisher.

A CIP record for this book is available from the British Library

ISBN 1-85375-298-3

Cover picture courtesy of George Riedel
Cover design: Bob Eames

Printed and bound in China

CONTENTS

INTRODUCTION
6

CHAPTER ONE
THE MAKING OF BRANDY
12

CHAPTER TWO
FRENCH BRANDIES
40

CHAPTER THREE
SPANISH BRANDIES
134

CHAPTER FOUR
ITALIAN BRANDIES
158

CHAPTER FIVE
BRANDIES FROM AROUND THE WORLD
186

CHAPTER SIX
THE TASTING OF BRANDY
240

GLOSSARY
249

INDEX
253

CLASSIC BRANDY

INTRODUCTION

WHY BRANDY?

First because I like the stuff, not, I hope to excess, but quite genuinely. To paraphrase the old song: 'I love brandy in the springtime I love brandy in the fall'. I sip brandy of an evening, I drink it as a long drink the year-round, with dry ginger in the winter, with a neutral fizz (like Perrier) in the summer, but however diluted the drink I'm always acutely conscious of the quality of the spirit in the glass.

For there's more to my interest than mere adoration. This book is, I hope, much more than a directory backed up by technical explanations. It's a conscious attempt to persuade readers that there's more to brandy than they had thought. For far too long the name has been used in two totally distinct contexts. It can either be the name for a distinguished spirit – almost inevitably cognac or perhaps armagnac – lovingly sipped, mostly by elderly gentlemen with broad purple noses, from massive balloon-shaped glasses, or for a mass of indifferent spirits used as mixers with everything from lemon juice to Coca-Cola without much thought to the quality of the brandy. There is nothing in between.

Opposite
This alluring Art Deco femme fatale invites us to a drink of Comandon and sets the pace for late 19th century brandy advertising.

INTRODUCTION

In this book I'm trying to establish a much more subtle hierarchy, to persuade readers that there are interesting qualities to be found in brandies from a dozen different countries, be they Spain, Israel or Armenia – all worthy of consideration as spirits in their own right. Obviously I start with cognac – and armagnac – because they remain the source of the very finest brandies, but if I can persuade you to take seriously brandies from outside the traditional areas, then I'll have succeeded in my self-imposed task.

CLASSIC BRANDY

WHAT'S 'CLASSIC'? WHAT'S 'BRANDY'?

Older readers may remember a favourite radio programme of mine, 'The Brains Trust'. Among the regular participants was Professor CEM Joad who became famous for his remark 'it depends what you mean by' – whatever subject was on the table. My reaction when confronted with the apparently simple title *Classic Brandy* was similar to Professor Joad's because both words contain traps, albeit different ones.

The word brandy covers a multitude of spirits distilled not just from grapes but from almost every known variety of fruit, from quince to cherry. For reasons of space as much as anything else I have had to confine myself to brandies distilled from grapes. Unfortunately the term 'grape brandy' is also used to describe cheap spirits which consist merely of neutral alcohol flavoured with aromatic grape spirit. To exclude such imitations I have confined myself to brandies the contents of which have been distilled directly from the grape. These, and these alone, produce the finest brandies, the only ones whose qualities change and expand for many decades when they are matured in wood.

But to complicate matters further I have included 'pomace' brandies, those distilled from the 'lees', the skins and pips which remain after the juice has been extracted during the wine-making process. These spirits are better known as *marc* in

INTRODUCTION

France, *grappa* in Italy (and now in the United States), *bagaceira* in Portugal and so on. They have been made for centuries in most traditional wine-growing regions to provide a drop of winter warmth – a dash of grappa in the coffee is a sensible habit in northern Italy. Moreover the wine-growers, being peasants, hated to see any part of their harvest going to waste, though they rarely sold such spirits outside their immediate neighbourhood.

In the past, because they were made from the leftovers of winemaking, and because of their perceived peasant origins, pomace brandies have been underrated. Not for these reasons but because the only grappas the average drinker came across were industrially made and thus rather characterless, their reputation was somewhat limited. However, they are now being increasingly appreciated and with good reason. The lees are so full of sugar and vinous goodies that these brandies have a delicious concentration of natural sweetness and intensity of fruit. Increasingly drinkers are coming to realise that pomace brandies can reflect the character of the grapes from which they are distilled, and some of them – notably the grappas made from single grape varieties – can be truly distinguished spirits.

This leaves a definition of the word 'classic', which has proved much more difficult. I see it as signifying that quality of spirit which reflects the true character both of the grapes from which it is made and of the country or region where it

CLASSIC BRANDY

is distilled. But this definition is rather restrictive since each region often has a number of different distillation traditions. And such a strict definition would also exclude quite a few well-known brands which don't happen to reflect the best examples of that region but which are better known than more authentic examples of the distiller's art from the same region. So, and purely for the purposes of this book, I have taken 'classic' to mean either 'well-known' or 'authentic' – or both! I have also attempted to include details from every notable producer, even those who did not reply to my publisher's repeated request for information. But the non-repliers can't really complain if the information on their brands is less complete – and possibly less accurate and up to date – than that provided by more co-operative firms.

My more specific definitions are orthodox enough, but where I find myself differing most obviously from previous works on the subject – including my own – is in the emphasis placed on different types of brandy. In the past cognac and, to a lesser extent, armagnac have formed the bulk of any guide to brandy. In compiling this book I have found so much of interest in other brandy-making countries that the non-French sections now account for the biggest single section of this book. In a way this is a tribute to the producers of cognac, if only because until recently most distillers the world over used the word 'cognac' or

INTRODUCTION

its local equivalent to describe their offerings. But today, although the pupils have never succeeded in producing brandies comparable with the finest cognacs, they can certainly compete honourably – and only too successfully so far as cognac is concerned – on what might be described as the lower slopes of the brandy mountain: those brandies designed to be mixed and consumed as long drinks, rather than the classier minority worthy to be nosed and sipped with care and loving appreciation.

And finally I must declare an interest. Since 1996 I have had the honour of chairing the International Spirits Challenge and so I naturally believe that the medals (and above all the trophies) delivered by the distinguished judges I have assembled are worth far more than those distributed by other competitions. This is not just egotism. So far as I know, the ISC is the only event of its kind in the world which combines two crucial attributes: it is not sponsored by any company involved with the production of spirits and its decisions are reached by panels of specialist judges. So I have naturally highlighted only the awards granted by the ISC.

NOTE: Throughout the book the term 'percentage alcohol' means precisely that – not proof nor ABV.

THE MAKING OF BRANDY

A SHORT HISTORY OF DISTILLATION

It was probably the Ancient Egyptians who discovered that by heating flowers, berries, herbs or spices they could achieve a greater concentration of taste and flavour. They also probably discovered – the whole subject is still a matter of historical argument – that heating actually 'distilled' the raw material. That is, instead of the raw material simply being concentrated in the process, its most important ingredients emerged at the top of the vessel in which it was being heated and could be captured by condensation in some type of hood above the stove, or 'still' as it is now known.

The reason why distillation is possible is simplicity itself; the chemical substances, 'esters' and other compounds responsible for the flavours in a brandy, boil at a lower temperature than water. Their fumes then rise above the still and can be captured – originally in a leather

Opposite
The Ancient Egyptians may well have invented distillation, though only to produce perfumes and medicines.

Chapter One

hood, then in the sort of copper globe still generally used – and subsequently cooled so that they return to a liquid form.

Throughout classical times, indeed until the early Middle Ages, the raw materials used did not include wine (in India even rice was used), and the resulting distillate – the aroma-laden vapours from the stove – was probably employed solely to make perfumes and medicines. We know that the distillation process was in use as early as the third or fourth century AD through a book attributed to this time on 'burners and other chemical instruments' by one Zozimus Thebanus. In this treatise he describes stills of different types he had seen in a temple near Memphis in Egypt – which illustrates the point that distillates were used mainly for religious and medicinal purposes.

Our knowledge of distillation – like so many technical advances from classical times – is due to the Arabs, who preserved so much ancient learning. Indeed until recently it was assumed that it was the Arabs who had invented the process of distillation and we continue to use words of Arabic origin for the still – alambic – and for the distillate – alcohol. At some unknown point there was a breakthrough and it was discovered that grapes and other fruits could produce an agreeably palatable spirit. By the 13th century we find a Franciscan monk based in Majorca, Ramon Lull (a name often translated

THE MAKING OF BRANDY

into Raymond Lulle), recommending the use of both red and white wine, provided that they were of good quality, in order to get desirable distillates. He had also grasped a point which remains central to the art of distillation to this day; that to retain as much of the quality of the original raw material as possible it should be heated over a gentle fire and must not be overly 'rectified' or purified by passing it too often through the still.

By the late 13th century the use of brandy, *aqua vitae,* literally 'the water of life', for pleasurable drinking, had been lauded by Arnoldo da Villanova, a leading doctor to three popes and the Holy Roman Emperor Frederick II, 'Stupor Mundi', the 'wonder of the world' as he was known to contemporaries. And by the end of the 14th century the Imperial authorities were using the phrase *Geprant Wein*, or 'burnt wine', to describe the spirit they were either banning or taxing. This was later transmuted by the Dutch into *brandewijn* and then by the English into brandy.

These political powers were also setting an important precedent, that of exploiting brandy as a useful source of tax revenue. Over the years governments in most brandy-drinking countries have gone a long way to killing the goose that was already laying golden eggs, through the imposition of heavy taxation. The Australians in the 1970s, the French government under President Mitterrand – ironically himself a native

Classic Brandy

THE MAKING OF BRANDY

of the Cognac region – followed by the Spanish government in the 1980s, have all greatly (and probably permanently) reduced brandy consumption by sharply increasing duties.

But long before M Mitterrand, the best brandies had been transformed into something rich and rare. By the end of the 16th century an Italian author (Vittorio Siri of Parma) had described the sequence of drinks to be followed in a dinner party as 'proceeding by degrees from common wines to brandy'. Clearly by then brandy had become what it still remains to this day, the most suitable and most noble of climaxes to the finest of dinner parties.

Opposite
The classical lines and grand design of this 1930s Rouyer ad show that, by this time, brandy had become part of the élite in the drink world.

THE RAW MATERIAL

Distillation is invariably the second stage in the process of transforming a raw material into spirit. What the distiller needs is a fermented product – made from grain for whisky production and wine for brandy as I have defined it – the alcoholic strength of which is greatly increased by distillation. As with any other wine or spirit the quality of the final product vitally depends on the quality of the raw material involved, for the very simple reason that distillation concentrates the defects as well as the qualities in the wine being used. With brandy the choice of grape variety is a complicated business, involving

Classic Brandy

THE MAKING OF BRANDY

the right balance of fruit and acid and the capacity to age gracefully in the oak casks which alone can allow brandy to mature. The traditional answer, not only in Cognac and Armagnac but also, increasingly, in regions like Catalonia and northern Portugal, is to use relatively neutral grape varieties high in acidity as the basis for brandies. The disadvantage of using more heavily flavourful varieties (of which muscat is the most obvious example) is that you end up with brandies which are too distinctive, too marked by the characteristics of the original grape variety. In wine this may be a good thing but the concentration involved in distillation inevitably means that it is very difficult to make an acceptable product from a strongly flavoured grape variety. Such brandies will also lack the proper balance of fruit, wood and structure.

As a result, the primary quality of the wine – apart from it being free of the defects which are multiplied by the distillation process – is that it should be properly acidic. This creates the paradox, in France anyway, that years like 1963 and 1968 which were disastrous for winemaking because of excess acidity (especially in Bordeaux a mere 80 miles south of Cognac) produced some distinguished brandies both in Cognac and Armagnac. Conversely 1989, a year which produced fat, fruity wines, posed major problems for the distillers and led the Cognaçais to greatly improve their wine making.

Opposite
Magical moments in the life-cycle of the vine – (bottom) the 'first growth' when the buds appear, in March or April, depending on the climate and the grape variety. Three months or so later comes the 'flowering' (top), a sort of puberty when the grapes take on their final form.

19

Classic Brandy

Grapes are complex fruits, and ideally the acidity should be balanced – as it is with the Folle Blanche grape – by a certain concentration of fruit. Nevertheless modern cognac is almost invariably distilled from the Ugni Blanc, one of the most neutral of all white grape varieties. But nonetheless it contains enough of the right stuff, the 'congeners', fatty acids and other impurities, to produce the finest of all brandies. The term congeners covers a multitude of substances found in wines and spirits; among which are both 'ethyl' and 'fusel' alcohols, subtle compounds which greatly affect the flavour of the final spirit.

DISTILLATION

Opposite
Classic pot-stills in burnished copper set into brickwork at the Château de Beaulon, south-west of Cognac.

However it is carried out, distillation remains essentially a simple process; 'simply controlled evaporation' as one expert put it to me. It is a physical process rather than a chemical one, which involves separating the alcohol and other impurities in the wine from the water which forms the bulk of its constituent parts. Simply described then, distillation consists of heating the

The Making of Brandy

Classic Brandy

The Making of Brandy

Left
The vineyards belonging to Camus in the rolling countryside of the Borderies north of Cognac produce very special, very nutty cognacs.

CLASSIC BRANDY

wine, or any other fermented liquid, and then capturing the alcoholic fumes once the raw material reaches 78.3 degrees centigrade, the boiling point of alcohol. Of course an infinite number of distinctions have emerged in the course of history. These started with the type of still – the traditional pot-still or the more industrial continuous Coffey still – which themselves entail innumerable complexities and variations.

But it gradually emerged, as Raymond Lulle had already noted in the 13th century, that there was a crucial balance to be observed; the more complete and therefore rigorous the distillation process, the less interesting the resultant distillate, since, by definition, it contained fewer of the impurities which give spirits their character. The less often the wine was distilled and the lower the strength of the final spirit, the better the brandy. Moreover the stronger the original alcoholic strength of the spirit as it emerged from the still, the fiercer the attack on the palate. Indeed Cognac rose to fame because the grapes grown on the slopes round the town had only to be distilled twice to produce a wholesome and drinkable spirit, whereas those from rival grape-growing regions in France had to be distilled half a dozen or more times. In the process of losing their impurities, they also lost almost all of their original character.

At the relatively low strengths at which brandy

THE MAKING OF BRANDY

is distilled in Cognac (up to 70 per cent alcohol) or Armagnac (where it can be as low as 52 per cent), the concentration which is at the heart of the process allows all the important elements in the original raw material to be retained. The impurities include hundreds of different ingredients, and the use of spectra-chromatographs has revealed not only their number, but the very different relative importance they can enjoy; a high concentration of one substance need not change the perceived taste or aromas of the brandy, while a minuscule amount of another can have the most extraordinary effects, for good or ill.

The actual amount of solid matter is very small (a maximum of 2 per cent) but the difference in the character of the spirit, its need for long maturation, and the resulting complexity of the mature spirit are amazing. Inevitably complexity brings its own risks in terms of impurities which are made more obvious and concentrated through the process of distillation. Nevertheless, the lower the percentage strength of the wine being used the better, simply because, if you take a wine of, say 9 per cent alcohol – the average in Cognac – the distillation process will multiply its alcoholic content eight times, essentially by the removal of the water in the wine. Whereas a wine of 11 per cent alcohol, like those used by the Spaniards, will be concentrated only six or seven times.

CLASSIC BRANDY

POT-STILLS

*Opposite
Sometimes useful
means beautiful,
as it does here
with a classic
condenser used to
cool the newly-
distilled brandy
which emerges
into the little
pail at the foot
of the pedestal.*

This is the original form of still, a pot filled with wine and then heated. The alcohol fumes are trapped at the top of the vessel and cooled. The word 'pot' is entirely appropriate, since the vessels are usually bulbous-shaped, if only to ensure that the fermenting liquid can swirl around within the still. Until the 19th century, it was the only type available but was soon replaced by the continuous Coffey still for the production of all brandies except the very best. The reason was purely economic; the pot-still is far less efficient than a continuous still because it distils in batches, each of which has to be heated, so it uses far more fuel and, almost inevitably, the fermented wine has to be distilled twice to produce a properly concentrated spirit. Yet the ability to control the process and retain the precious substances which will give body and flavour to the final product mean that virtually all the world's finest spirits (apart from armagnac) come from pot-stills, including the best offerings from brandy-makers the world over. This preference is not confined to grapes, malt whisky and Calvados are also produced in pot-stills.

Inevitably, in a piece of apparatus invented at least 700 years ago, certain elements have been standardised, while others have developed local variants. The vessels are almost invariably made of copper, which is a virtually neutral metal and

THE MAKING OF BRANDY

thus does not damage the spirit. Chemically the copper helps to fix the fatty acids in the wine, as well as any sulphurous products in the alcoholic vapour that would harm the quality of the spirit. So far as grape spirits are concerned, they are heated from outside the still, although gas, which provides the desirable qualities of uniform and controllable heat, has usually replaced wood or coal as a fuel.

The differences appear most obviously in the size of the vessel and the mechanisms used to trap the fumes. The size has increased over the years, although the size of stills used in the second distillation – *deuxième chauffe* – in Cognac are strictly limited to 25 hectolitres; the equivalent of about 3000 bottles and a tribute to the role it plays in concentrating the inherent qualities of the wine, qualities which would be somewhat lost in a bigger vessel. This particular size seems to have been arrived at by a matter of historical trial and error with no convincing scientific evidence.

The shape of the head of the still and the duct leading to the cooler also have a part to play. The older type, called *tête de*

CLASSIC BRANDY

maure, literally 'moor's head', but in fact looking more like a cartoon animal with a sharp beak, retained more of the impurities, and thus produced a richer, less uniform brandy than the modern *col de cygne* or 'swan's neck' which provides an infinitely smoother path for the brandy than the older, more angular designs.

Cognac, and other pot-still brandies, are distilled twice to emerge at about 70 per cent alcohol. The first distillation produces what is known as the *brouillis*, about 30 per cent alcohol, which contains all the essential elements for the final product. The second distillation, known as *la bonne chauffe* in Cognac, merely concentrates and separates the crucial elements.

Control is largely exercised in the decision as to when to start to keep the spirit, at what point to stop discarding the relatively high-strength *têtes*, the 'heads' – the first drops to flow from the still – and when to cut the *queues* or 'tails', the

Right
Crucial elements in brandy-making: filtering the newly-distilled spirit and...

The Making of Brandy

final spirit to emerge. These are lower in alcohol, richer and contain more of the desirable congeners, but, as a natural corollary, they also contain more impurities.

The speed of distillation is also a crucial factor, and this is where brandies distilled in a pot-still enjoy an enormous advantage, for they enable the distiller to control the process more accurately. By varying the temperature the distiller can maximise the length of time required and thus extract the greatest possible proportion of the desirable ingredients in the wine. In that sense distillation is like stewing fruit, where the longer and slower the cooking process the more concentrated the final product and the fuller it will be of flavour.

Above
...*measuring its alcoholic strength.*

Some distillers (notably the Californians), anxious to produce a light style of brandy, make considerable efforts to reduce the proportion of fusel alcohols; the cleaner the original wine and the less contact it has had with skins, the lower the levels. But fusels are greatly cherished by other distillers because in time, and this is the crucial point about maturation, they will change into the desirable compounds known as esters.

CLASSIC BRANDY

Unfortunately a brandy with too high a proportion of fusel alcohols will come through with a disagreeable tarry, overly grapey, rasping taste.

In a pot-still the ethyl alcohols emerge as part of the heads, the first spirit through the still, and the distiller must capture them without also including the less desirable compounds which emerge at the same time. The less volatile chemical constituents of the wine will surface late in the distillation process, and will thus form part of the tails. This fraction is discarded both because it is low in strength and because it inevitably contains undesirable compounds. The *têtes* are usually redistilled because they are too strong and thus too neutral. They can, however, be useful in a bad year when the wines lack acidity and the brandies are liable to be bland and characterless.

There are many other variations of the distillation process. Should the wine be preheated? Should it be distilled on its lees? The answer to the first is probably yes, unless you are anxious to get a relatively neutral spirit; to the second, yes, again to provide additional richness. Nevertheless modern chemistry is only now beginning to grapple with the complexities involved, thus ensuring that the personality of the product, and thus of the firm selling it, is retained; a guarantee enhanced by the mere use of a pot-still.

Opposite

In Armagnac they have developed their own type of continuous still with only a few 'plates' to produce a relatively low-strength brandy.

The Making of Brandy

Coffey Stills

In 1827 Robert Stein, a forebear of the Haig whisky distilling family, patented an apparatus which distilled a continuous stream of beer into potable spirit. The device was naturally inspected by customs officials, including an Irishman, Aeneas Coffey who, in 1830–31, adapted it to use wine rather than beer as a raw material. Since then, somewhat unfairly, it has been called the Coffey still. Its introduction inaugurated a new era in the history of spirits. It involved a clear distinction between continuously distilled spirits which were mass-produced, and those, mostly using pot-stills, which were what the French would call *artisanale* or 'hand-crafted'. For the Coffey still, while far more efficient, is more brutal in its handling of the raw material than is a pot-still. And in most continuous stills (though not in the special type used in armagnac) the hot wine is mixed with steam to help extract the alcohol, thus further coarsening the resulting spirit.

Classic Brandy

A Coffey still uses two columns. In one, wine is preheated in a heat exchanger. It is then introduced at the top of a 'fractionating' column, so called because it divides the wine into fractions, and then lets it trickle down through a series of perforated plates. The alcohol is released when the wine hits the hot plates in a cloud of steam rising from the base of the column. The (lighter) alcohol fumes then emerge from the top of the column. The 'aldehydes' and other highly volatile elements pass to the very top of the column, while the desirable fusel alcohols are concentrated about four plates from the top.

As can be imagined, there are numerous variations on the basic process. The most important concerns the number of plates in the distilling column. The more there are, the more highly rectified is the resulting spirit, and the fewer impurities it contains. At the limit a 100 per cent pure spirit will be totally characterless. But even a spirit which emerges as 95 per cent pure has a surprising amount of character. At the other extreme, the brandies distilled to a mere 52 per cent in the stills traditionally used in Armagnac retain a disproportionate percentage of the chemical ingredients (notably the congeners) of the original wine. Of course there are many other ways in which wines are distilled into brandy, but these are local variants and are described in the sections on individual regions.

The Making of Brandy

Ageing

Distillation is only the first stage in the production of a fine spirit (as opposed to an industrial-type alcohol). The more interesting chemical reactions occur when the raw spirit is matured in wood, almost invariably oak, which itself usually comes from France or the United States. Brandy can also be given an artificial oakiness by addition of oak chips, what the French call *boisé,* which artificially speed up the ageing process.

Ageing in oak is a vital element in the production of fine brandies. Originally it was used for purely practical reasons – distillers were lucky that oak, which offers an ideal material for ageing brandy, grew near many distilleries – yet it remains the ideal container, performing both physical and chemical functions in the maturation process. Indeed, the final product is a blend of the original spirit and the qualities imparted by the oak, and the balance between the two plays a crucial role in its quality. The balance is a delicate one; obviously the newer the wood in which the spirit is stored and the longer it remains in wood the greater its influence. To maximise the wood's influence on the spirit, most serious brandies are matured in relatively small oak casks; in Cognac, for example, these hold 350 litres. But to achieve a balanced result, the brandies cannot be left in new casks for too

Classic Brandy

The Making of Brandy

long (rarely more than a year) because otherwise they would retain too much of the woodiness so often encountered in over-oaked wines. They are then transferred to older casks for the rest of their maturation process. This can vary from two years in all for the youngest armagnacs, (three for cognac) to ten times as long for the finest brandies.

Physically, oak is hard, supple and water-tight – thus making it suitable for storage and transportation. It is also dense – thus allowing only a slow evaporation. There are many variations in its overall effect; American oak can impart bitter tastes, particularly to cognac, while oak from the forests round the Adriatic or 'Trieste oak' can be too hard. The physical properties ensure a steady, controlled continuation of the evaporation process which started so fast in the still. The stately pace of the evaporation ensures that none of the precious aromatic qualities in the spirit are lost in the process.

But, inevitably, the evaporation involves the loss of alcohol. In dry cellars more liquid is lost than alcoholic strength; in the more desirable, damper cellars the reverse is

Left
The dignity of an old-fashioned chai. *Note the bigger casks on the gallery used to blend and dilute the cognacs.*

CLASSIC BRANDY

Opposite
The oak trees in the Tronçais forest, in the very centre of France, grow straight and so slowly that they can be used to make casks only when they are centenarians.

the case. However, even in a good cellar over half the original volume – as against a mere 6–7 per cent of the original alcoholic strength – will have been lost after the brandy has been in cask for 15 years.

Two-thirds of oak is composed of elements which are chemically neutral, so their only effect on the maturation process is physical; that is, they allow a tiny, if regular, supply of air to percolate through to the spirit. Fortunately most of the soluble elements which would introduce bitter elements into the brandy are eliminated by the sun and the rain when the wood is dried, as it should be, in the open air (wood dried in a kiln does not lose all the undesirable elements).

Oak also has one crucial negative virtue; it contains little or none of the resinous substances found in species such as pine which could pollute the spirit with undesirable resinous tastes. It also has a number of positively useful elements; 'tannins', the best known, which comprise a mere 5 per cent of the wood and the equally vital but less appreciated 'lignins' at 23 per cent. But even the supposedly neutral hemi-cellulose which makes up much of the rest is useful. As it gradually dissolves in the maturing spirit, it provides the agreeable sweetness found in older brandies.

The tannins impart colour to spirit which was colourless when it emerged from the still, and at first they increase its bitterness. But after a few

years the molecules have enlarged, causing the flavour to mellow. The lignins' first impact is to bring an aroma of balsam wood. But when they break down they create the lovely vanilla and cinnamon overtones detectable in some brandies. The processes are slow, in cognac especially; the tannins only really start to build up after eight or more years. Although the brandy has absorbed the 'vanillins' within a few years, and the aldehydes reach their peak within 30 years, the volatile acids build up over the full 50 years that the best brandies remain in cask, although all the tannins and lignins have been absorbed within 30 or 35 years.

THE EUROPEAN UNION AND BRANDY

On 12th June 1989 the EEC promulgated a set of regulations covering the official definition of brandies within the community. Brandies were defined in one of three ways.

'Wine Spirit' must be produced by distillation (or redistillation) at less than 86 per cent alcohol by volume (abv) of wine, fortified or unfortified. Wine spirit also has to contain at least 125 grams per hectolitre of pure alcohol of volatile substances (other than ethyl and methyl alcohol) and a maximum of 200 grams of methyl alcohol per hectolitre.

THE MAKING OF BRANDY

'Brandy' or *Weinbrand* follows the definition of Wine Spirit but can be distilled at up to 94.8 per cent (abv). It has to contain 200 rather than 125 grams of volatile substances and must be aged for at least one year in oak receptacles or for at least six months in oak casks containing less than 1000 litres.

'Grape marc' or 'Grape marc spirit' has to be produced exclusively by the distillation of grape marc, with or without added water. A percentage of lees – which has not yet been fixed – can be added. The whole has to be distilled at below 86 per cent alcohol, so that the distillate retains the aromatic contents of the raw materials. The spirit has to contain a minimum of 140 grams per hectolitre of pure alcohol of volatile substances other than ethyl and methyl alcohol and a maximum of 1000 grams of methyl alcohol per hectolitre of pure alcohol. The term 'Grappa', which follows the definition of marc, covers only spirits produced in Italy.

CLASSIC BRANDY

FRENCH BRANDIES

COGNAC

Cognac has held the high ground as the world's finest brandy for over three hundred years. This superiority is firmly based on systematic exploitation by man of the region's natural advantages. As a result, the little town in western France – with only 5000 inhabitants at the time of its rise to fame – is better known than any other French place-name, except, of course, for Paris. The town remains compact, its heart a picturesque huddle of narrow streets bounded by often rather dilapidated warehouses. These are instantly recognisable because their roofs have invariably been blackened by the effect of a mould, *torula compniacensis richon*, which thrives on the aromatic fumes from hundreds of casks of maturing cognac.

Cognac's exploitation of its natural advantages started in the early Middle Ages, centuries before its first wines were distilled. Its position on the River Charente provided it with a major trade in

Opposite

Cognac as it was in the mid 19th century, a thriving, industrious town, as producer of its eponymous spirit.

CHAPTER TWO

salt, and then in wine from the slopes above the town, supplies of which helped to satisfy the insatiable English thirst during the centuries when the king of England also ruled over Aquitaine. Politically Cognac was also lucky. The French king Francis II was born in the town in 1492 and naturally favoured his birthplace. Moreover (and unlike Jarnac a few miles upstream, a major centre of Protestantism), Cognac was on the Catholic side during the wars of religion which raged through the 16th century.

But Cognac's breakthrough came thanks to the Dutch, who wanted *brandewijn* rather than wine for their sailors, and it was they who first bought the wine for distillation at home and then imported their own stills to distil the wine nearer the source. By the middle of the 17th century even the fine wines from the Champagnes [qv] were being used for distillation, because it had been realised that these wines produced pure brandies after only two distillations, while rival wines needed many more passes through the stills to eliminate nauseous impurities, which also removed their grapey characteristics.

Brandy from Cognac soon found a market which was to dominate the fine end of the trade for nearly three centuries, for it took only a few years for the London connoisseurs of the late 17th century to grasp the fact that brandy from Cognac ('Coniac', or 'Coniack' – spelling has

FRENCH BRANDIES

never been the strong suit of the British upper classes) was superior to that from bigger centres of the wine trade, like 'Nants' or La Rochelle, or Bordeaux, the source of another newly fashionable drink – mature claret.

In the following century the trade attracted a number of high-grade entrepreneurs, most importantly the former smuggler Jean Martell and Richard Hennessy, an Irish-born officer in

Left
Jean Martell, the former smuggler from the Channel Islands, founded one of Cognac's most venerable firms – helped by marriages to members of even older-established merchants.

the French army. These two men and the firms they founded helped to ensure that the basic quality of cognac has always been higher than that of any other distilled spirit – at the expense, perhaps, of a certain amount of the picturesque individuality attached to Armagnac.

The duopoly created by Messrs Martell and Hennessy has been successfully challenged for any length of time only by two other firms: Courvoisier and Rémy Martin. Between them the Big Four now account for four-fifths of the cognac sold outside France (the French themselves are less concerned with quality than with price, buying mostly cheap, raw supermarket cognacs). In the late 1980s even these rose rapidly in price because the growers, particularly in the outer sub-regions, took over-enthusiastic advantage of the premiums paid by the EEC for pulling up surplus vines. The resulting shortage, especially of mature cognacs, was exacerbated by the damage caused by *eutypiose*, a fungal disease that rots the wood of the vine.

Sadly, cognac has had every sort of problem over the past few years. The major firms became arrogant, refusing to give precise ages to their brandies – which put them at a major disadvantage compared with the purveyors of malt whiskies. In addition the latter were far cheaper to produce because barley costs so much less than grapes or wine. Two of the big four, Martell and Courvoisier, have seen their former cognac bases reduced to

FRENCH BRANDIES

mere production and ageing units, with the major decisions being taken far away at the headquarters of the groups (Seagram and Allied-Domecq respectively) to which they belong.

To make matters worse, until a few years ago the cognac producers refused even to consider the idea that their precious brandy should be promoted as a long drink. Yet there was a perfectly honourable tradition of a late-night 'b & s' – brandy and soda – in Britain, and of *fine a l'eau* – with still water – in France. They refused to admit that the bulk of their production was being drunk either with ice on Chinese dinner tables or with Coca-Cola and

Below
A Croizet ad portrays Arcadia in the heart of the Grande Champagne.

Classic Brandy

other impurities in the United States, especially among the poorest – predominantly Afro-American – drinkers who accounted for most of consumption of the basic VS brandies.

The only advantage of the region's trials and tribulations – which in reality started with the first oil crisis of 1973 and were merely papered over by the boom in sales to the Far East in the late 1980s and early 90s – is that dozens of small distillers who used to sell to the bigger firms found themselves with stocks of older brandies and started to sell them under their own name, providing discerning buyers with a range of products far greater than ever before.

Despite its problems – which resulted in rioting and an expensive restructuring plan financed by the French taxpayer – Cognac retains enormous assets. All cognac passes the great test of any brandy, its capacity to retain so much of the character of the original fruit. But, naturally, Cognac's fame reposes most securely on its finest products. After 30 years or more in oak casks, brandies from the circle of chalk slopes known as the Champagnes offer an incomparable richness of fruit, balanced by an equally unique elegance and delicacy. But the Cognac region also includes two other sub-regions

FRENCH BRANDIES

whose products are both superior to any other brandies from outside Cognac (except for Armagnac): the Borderies, and the Fins Bois round Cognac's sister town, Jarnac, a few miles further up the River Charente.

Cognac's natural advantages start with its *terroir*, that untranslatable French term summing up a mix of soil, sub-soil, climate, and all the other geographical and climatic factors that affect the product of the vine. Legally, cognac can

Below
Martell's vineyards are absolutely typical of the rolling countryside round Cognac.

Classic Brandy

Opposite
The rings around Cognac form the different sub-regions of the Cognac appellation.

only be produced in a strictly defined region round the River Charente extending inland from the estuary of the Gironde and the Bay of Biscay towards Angoulême, 50 miles inland. This town originally made its name from the brandies produced on a semicircle of chalky slopes to the south of Cognac and Jarnac. Solely because of the differences in *terroir*, after a few years in cask, brandies made from the same type of grape, the same wine, distilled in the same stills, being matured in the same casks, take on very different characteristics.

Historically the Cognac area was divided into dozens of different regions, but, effectively, there are now only five that matter. These form irregular rings round Cognac – although today very few cognac grapes are grown west of the town except on the islands of Ré and Oléron where they acquire a salty tang much appreciated by tourists. In ascending order of quality they go from the Bois Communs – or Ordinaires – up through the Bon Bois, the Fins Bois to the Borderies, and the two Champagnes, Petite and Grande. The outer circle, the Petite Champagne, is composed of Santonian chalk, named after Saintonge, the old name for the region. The inner circle, the Grande Champagne, has slopes of an even more special type of chalk, the Campanian named after the Campagna, the chalky countryside north of Rome (Fine Champagne cognacs are blended from the two

FRENCH BRANDIES

areas, with at least half Grande Champagne). The Borderies, a small, clayey-chalky rectangle north of Cognac, produces special and unmistakable brandies, offering the intensity of fruity nuttiness found in fine tawny port, while the best brandies from the Fins Bois which surround the Champagnes produce a light, flowery, elegant type of brandy, associated in the old days with the town of Jarnac. All these

FRENCH BRANDIES

brandies reflect more of the original grape, they are subtler, richer, finer, than brandies made anywhere else in the world.

Terroir includes the climate as well as soil. And the Charente is blessed with an equable climate: long – not too hot – summer days (outside Cognac itself) which ensure that the grapes do not ripen too quickly and are reasonably fruity even when they are still relatively acid and thin in alcohol. Ideally the grapes should contain between 8 and 9 per cent potential alcohol. If they are stronger, then the final brandy tends to be flabby and does not contain nearly as strong a concentration of the qualities found in the original fruit (for the obvious reason that a wine of 12 per cent distilled to 70 per cent alcohol is only concentrated six times, whereas a wine of 9 per cent alcohol is concentrated nearly eight times). At the other end of the scale, grapes containing less than 8 per cent alcohol will simply be too green to have developed the right potential aromas.

The makers of cognac are working with a limited palette. In the 18th century much brandy was distilled from the Colombard grape still extensively grown in Armagnac, and in the 19th century it was made from a particularly aromatic variety, the Folle Blanche. But this proved to be liable to rot when grafted vines were planted following the *phylloxera vastatrix* epidemic and today virtually all the wine used for cognac comes from the same, rather

Opposite
A bunch of the Folle Blanche, the deliciously floral variety responsible for the finest 19th century cognacs but which proved too susceptible to rot when grafted onto American root stock after the phylloxera *epidemic.*

characterless, grape, known variously as the Ugni Blanc or Saint Emilion.

The wine is fermented without using sulphur, which would emerge as an undesirable element in the final brandy, and is distilled as soon as possible after fermentation, preferably before Christmas but certainly before the end of March following fermentation. The copper Cognac pot-stills and the distillation process have not changed much over the years. The only change has been in the method of heating. The source of heat remains external, but first coal and, more recently, natural gas, have replaced wood for firing the stills. This provides an ideal source of heat, controllable and above all uniform, ensuring that the brandy is not burnt.

Every serious firm has its own style, much of which depends on the cut-off point when the distiller returns the final flow (the *queues*) to be redistilled. So a house like Bisquit, looking for a fruity style even in its VS, will leave the tap running – and thus extract lower-strength brandy – longer than, say, Martell, which is looking for a relatively neutral raw material. The difference is not great, a matter of half a degree or so, but it counts.

Newly distilled cognac is pretty rough stuff, and not only because of its strength, which is around 70 per cent alcohol. It lacks a crucial

French Brandies

dimension which can be provided only by its storage in the small oak casks which allow the subtle chemical process of maturation: the brandy slowly absorbing the tannins and vanillins from the oak.

The major cognac firms know this perfectly well and have taken care to control the manufacture of their casks very closely. Indeed until recently Hennessy and Rémy Martin owned Taransaud and Séguin-Moreau, two of France's biggest firms of coopers. All cognac is matured in French oak, but that from the Tronçais forest in the centre of France in the Bourbonnais, west of Burgundy, differs from the

Above
Under a fifth of these oaks from the Tronçais can be used to make casks.

alternative wood from the Limousin near Limoges. Rémy uses Limousin oak, rich in tannin, to accelerate the maturation of its Champagne brandies, mostly destined to be sold younger than purists would advise. Martell, by contrast, in its continuing search for a certain austerity of style, uses Tronçais oak which is tougher and less generous with its tannins.

The choice between new and old oak is even more fundamental. Those houses, most obviously Delamain, looking for a light style, use none, but most other firms keep their newly distilled brandies in new oak for up to a year. At the other extreme Frapin, which sells mostly brandies from well-placed estates in the Grande Champagne, characterful enough to be able to absorb a lot of tannin, keeps its brandies in new wood for up to two years.

The maturing brandies are then housed in hundreds of warehouses or *chais* in and around Cognac. For obvious reasons of transport convenience, the older cellars were all situated on the banks of the Charente. As a result they were

FRENCH BRANDIES

damp, which was a good thing, since a damp cellar reduces the strength rather than the volume of the spirit, while evaporation is faster

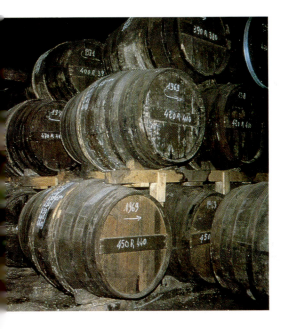

Left
In the cellars of Ragnaud-Sabourin, each 300 litre cask has an individual identity.

(and accompanied by a slower loss of strength) in a dry cellar, resulting in an undesirably harsh style of brandy. During previous centuries the 'Early Landed, Late Bottled' brandies destined for the aristocratic end of the British market were matured in equally damp warehouses near the docks in London and Bristol. Between 20 and 40

CLASSIC BRANDY

years later they were bottled and sold under the names both of the supplier and the merchant. Even today all the cognac houses avoid dry cellars. Indeed, when Bisquit moved from the banks of the Charente to a new site on the slopes some miles away, it ensured that the new *chais* were properly moisturised.

Over the years a hierarchy has emerged within Cognac, based on a combination of the geographical origin of the grapes and the length of time the cognac has spent in cask. But even the most basic cognac, the VS (still better known under its historic XXX title) cannot contain any brandy less than three years old, while the VSOP (originally named after the Very Special Old Pale brandies sold in London in Victorian times) cannot be less than five years old. But the authorities lose track of brandies after they are ten years old, and buyers have to rely on the reputation of the firm when choosing between the proliferation of superior grades: the Napoleons, the Extras, the XOs, and the like. For these names provide no guarantee of style – or quality for that matter – and there is a considerable variation in the age and quality of the cognacs involved.

Nevertheless brandies from the Fins Bois or the Borderies are at their best after less than two decades and even those from the Champagnes do not develop any further after 40 years or so in wood (forget the cobwebs, age-snobbery is just

FRENCH BRANDIES

that, snobbery). But nevertheless the finest cognacs need at least 20 years to develop. Only after two decades in cask do they develop the lovely ripe, rich feel the Cognaçais call *rancio*. This bears no relation to the artificial richness and woodiness imparted by the addition of caramel, or of the *boisé*, the wood chips, used to provide artificial age to some brandies. Chemically *rancio* derives from the oxidation of the fatty acids in the spirit, producing the 'ketones' which produce the richness felt on the palate with such brandies.

This richness emerges in a complex series of sensations on the nose and palate. 'Rankness, a special character of fullness and richness' was the unflattering description given by Charles Walter Berry, the wine merchant who was Britain's leading cognac connoisseur between the wars. This richness, allied to a certain mild cheesiness in the nose, reminds some tasters of Roquefort cheese. But to Anglo-Saxon palates the richness, depth and diversity of *rancio* brings forth memories of

Above
Cognac distilled, amazingly, just as Nelson was beating the French navy at Trafalgar and kept these many years in wicker-covered glass 'bonbonnes' in the venerable cellars of AE Dor, in Jarnac.

CLASSIC BRANDY

the rich fruit cakes traditionally made at Christmas. They are heavy, yes, but their smell and taste reflect the extraordinary variety of their ingredients, including candied fruits – apricot often stands out – as well as a richness from the sultanas, and a nuttiness from the almonds and walnuts in the mix.

Traditional English drinkers (like Berry and his customers) rather scorned the richness of the *rancio*. They preferred the lighter, more elegant 'Early Landed, Late Bottled' brandies produced by firms like Hine and Delamain. But, recently, even these seem to have acquired a touch of the richness and complexity which, to many modern connoisseurs, is one of the essential ingredients to a truly great cognac.

For some houses, the most important stylistic weapons they wield are the additives they employ. They all use a tiny quantity of caramel to ensure that the colour does not vary from cask to cask. Because it has no effect on the taste, you could, in theory, have a dry, dark-brown brandy. But because buyers are conditioned to associate brown with sweetness, the houses use colour as a signal of taste; especially to the Chinese, great cognac drinkers, who love the cognac with which they accompany their meals to be rich and thus, by association, dark and sweet.

To sweeten and enrich young cognacs you need sugar syrup, much used by some firms to provide a notably rounded style. Both caramel and sugar syrup are legal, above board and freely discussed additives. But there is one unregulated, largely unmentioned but extremely important style-bender; the *boisé* discussed in the previous section of this book – oak chips soaked in old cognac and left in the cask for months or years. To aficionados the richness it imparts to the brandy is rather hard and tannic and cannot be mistaken for real *rancio*.

Recently some cognacs have reverted to their older, heavier, stickier, and browner style, in response to demand from the Far East, most notably from the Japanese and from the prosperous Chinese communities throughout South East Asia, who drink cognac with water throughout their meals. Indeed the inhabitants of Hong Kong drink more cognac per head than anywhere else in the world, and the total consumption from the prosperous and thirsty Chinese there, and in Taiwan, Thailand, Singapore and Malaysia makes them the biggest single market for cognac.

But in recent years a younger generation, as so often happens, has abandoned the drinking habits of their parents. This trend, compounded by the Asian economic crisis of the late 1990s, sharply reduced consumption in the Far East. The only growth market appeared to be the range of richer cognacs designed to accompany cigars. Belatedly, the Cognaçais have been forced to promote their brandy as suitable for mixing.

Classic Brandy

FRENCH BRANDIES

As you can see from the Directory, many firms have introduced new, younger brandies to go with mixers. The Cognaçais have concentrated (unwisely to my mind) on tonic, albeit with some success, at least in the French market.

Nevertheless the Cognaçais still rely overmuch on glamour, mystique, their name and the guarantee it provides of superiority over brandies from any other source. The dominance of a handful of big firms, however reliable their products, has prevented cognac from developing the snob appeal required at a time when 'small is beautiful'. Some armagnacs still have this reputation largely because the Armagnaçais have never had the same commercial sense as the Cognaçais so there are no mass-production house styles. As a result, outside the Far East, cognac is on the decline, not only because of the world-wide swing away from heavier spirits in general and towards lighter ones such as vodka, but because most firms have not managed to inject any excitement into the business of buying or drinking cognac.

Historically, a few growers, notably the two branches of the Ragnaud family, had shown that there was a market for fine old brandies from individual estates in the heart of the Grande Champagne. Fortunately the Cognaçais have now recognised the need for single-vintage cognacs, an important marketing point since British drinkers in particular attach great importance to the idea

Opposite
Chinese interest in cognac dates back at least to the early 20th century. (The Robin family has now taken its expertise to California.)

Classic Brandy

Opposite
Beatrice Cointreau, chairman of the family firm of Frapin, in the family's historic offices in Segonzac, the heart of the Grande Champagne.

of a drink's vintage. New regulations, first introduced with the 1988 vintage, allow *millesimé* cognacs. A few houses – like Croizet and above all Hine – are now supplying such brandies and indeed cognac's future does seem to lie increasingly with the small quantities of the finest brandies sold by specialists.

Cognac – Regulations and Ages

Until it is blended and bottled, every vat or cask of cognac has an age attached to it. Cognacs are tagged with *Compte 00* when they have been distilled between the harvest and the following 31st March. At that point they are termed *Compte 0* cognacs (brandies distilled after 1st April are called *Compte 00* until the following 31st March).

From then on the *Comptes* move with the age: *Compte 1* refers to cognacs which are more than a year old on the 1st April of a given year etc. Until recently the *Compte* system stopped at year six, in fact brandies labelled *Compte 6* could be anything from six to a hundred years old. Stung by the ability of the distillers of malt whisky to offer spirits of a definite age, the *Compte* system has now been extended so that there is now a *Compte 10* indicating brandies which are more than ten years old.

Cognacs cannot be sold in France until they are at least *Compte 2* – and then they can be sold

CLASSIC BRANDY

only as VS (Very Special) or XXX. Most other major markets insist that their brandies be three years old or more.

To be called Reserve, VO (Very Old) or VSOP (Very Special Old Pale) the youngest brandy in a blend must be *Compte 4* – at least four and a half years old. To be called Extra, Napoleon, Vieux, Vieille Reserve or another name which implies that the cognac is old, the youngest spirit in the blend must be *Compte 6*. As from 2000, in a much needed regulation to prevent the looseness of the description on the past, any cognac calling itself XO will have to be at least *Compte 8*.

These regulations are still flexible enough to allow for an extraordinary degree of variation between the ages of brandies bearing the same indication of quality. In particular VSOP cognacs can vary between an average age of the minimum four years and a more acceptable and more rounded eight or nine, while XOs can be up to 25 years old – or so some producers will tell you, though you have no way of knowing whether they are telling the truth. Best to rely on your taste buds and on the reputation of the firm involved.

Until recently producers were not allowed to give their brandies a single vintage. The only ones available were the 'Early Landed Late Bottled' brandies which had been shipped to Britain soon after distillation and matured under the eagle eye of HM Customs & Excise, thus guaranteeing their age. But since 1988 cognac producers have been allowed to offer single-vintage cognacs provided that the French authorities are satisfied of their exact age. Judging by the number of single-vintage cognacs now on offer, either the authorities have been lax or the producers have kept very precise records of the contents of each of their casks. And to be fair, I haven't come across any instances of abuse of the new freedom; producers simply aren't going to risk their reputation by offering cognacs that are clearly younger than the date on the label.

Classic Brandy

Cognac Directory

Audry

A small firm with some of cognac's finest hidden treasures. A family firm founded back in 1878 it stopped selling any of its stock for several decades until 1976. As a result the present owner, Bernard Boisson, can now offer some of the most satisfying brandies in the region.

Opposite
Every wall throughout the Cognac region is plastered with advertising slogans that add a very distinct character to the area.

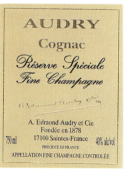

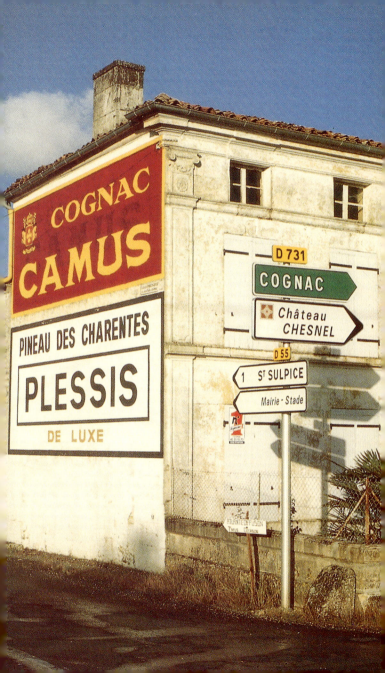

CLASSIC BRANDY

DANIEL BOUJU

A classic small grower-distiller in the heart of the Grande Champagne. The Allard family first grew grapes there in 1805 and distilled them. The family, now in its seventh generation, takes great care over every stage (including that rarity in the Charentes, hand-picking the grapes) and uses small pot-stills to get the most concentrated brandy possible. Uses only old wood and soon transfers to bigger casks to minimise the tannin. The result? Some distinguished cognacs ranging from a VSOP to an unfiltered Reserve Familiale.

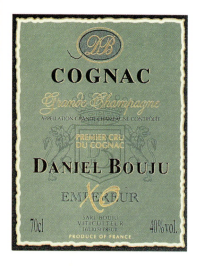

FRENCH BRANDIES

LOUIS BOURON
Based on the family property of Château de la Grange dating back to the 14th century, the firm has the peculiarity of offering only brandies made from grapes from their own estates in the Fins Bois, Petite Champagne and Borderies. VS, Très Vieille Reserve and an XO.

BOUTINET
A 26-hectare vineyard at Le Brissoneau, in the excellent north-eastern part of the Fins Bois which has been in the same family for nearly two centuries. The family offers a full range including a

CLASSIC BRANDY

vintage 1988, a good age for a Fin Bois. Also in the list is a 'Coeur de Fins Bois' which has been matured in very old oak. As a result it has little tannin and thus is suitable for long drinks.

FRENCH BRANDIES

MAISON BRILLET

A long-established family-owned firm with vineyards in the Champagnes which account for most of its grapes. An excellent range, culminating in the 50-year-old Heritage which is sold at its cask strength.

CAMUS

Family firm founded by Jean-Baptiste Camus, great-grandfather of the present chairman, Jean-Paul Camus. In the 1860s Jean-Baptiste had the bright idea of bringing together a group of growers and marketing their brandies under the name 'La Grande Marque'. Later he added his own name and since then the Grande Marque has taken a subordinate place. A century later the firm was

Above

The Chateau de Plessis, Camus' pride and joy in the Borderies.

CLASSIC BRANDY

restored to greatness through an alliance with Duty-Free Shoppers, a firm which dominated the highly profitable duty-free market in the Far East. Today their finest product is Chateau de Plessis, a rare and nutty rounded brandy from their own property in the Borderies.

CASTEL-SABLONS

Family firm in the southern part of the Fins Bois offering two very individual cognacs: the almost colourless Crystal Dry was one of the first to be designed for use as a base for cocktails, while the fearsomely strong (58 per cent alcohol) Brulot Charentais, named after the local speciality of the same name was designed to act as a pick-me-up (or let-me-fall-down) when ignited over a cup of coffee.

French Brandies

Chabanneau
Old brand owned by Camus [qv] and now used for speciality cognacs.

Château de Beaulon
The château itself was built in the late 15th century and is still in the heart of the Thomas family's 225-acre estate on the chalky pocket of soil near the estuary of the Gironde. A very integrated estate owned by Monsieur and Madame Christian Thomas which is best known for making some of the finest Pineaus de Charente. Unusually for the Charente, the vines are carefully, ecologically tended and the wines are well churned before distilling – which is done at the earliest possible moment to preserve the wine's freshness. All the brandies are much older than the legal minimum – and it shows. The VS is at least seven years old, the VSOP and Napoleon at least 12 and there are two specials, a 1976 and a Rare dating back to the early 20th century.

CLASSIC BRANDY

Below
Pierre Valet, the very model of the 19th century patriarch.

CHATEAU MONTIFAUD

One of the few firms in Cognac allowed to use the word 'Chateau.' An excellent 50-hectare property in the best part of the Petite Champagne which has been owned by the Vallet family for nearly two hundred years. Sensibly their ordinary cognacs are rather older than the official minimum age – even their VS is five years old. Naturally they also have some older brandies, including a delicious 1970, 'Cognac Grand Siècle' made from brandies between 20 and 25 years old – when they still retain some fruitiness and a really aged bottle given to visiting politicians (far too good for them, I say).

French Brandies

Courvoisier

The perennial outsider among the Big Four in the cognac business, this Jarnac-based firm has always been owned by outsiders; today it is a subsidiary of the British group, Allied Domecq. It was founded in the early 19th century but came to the fore only when it exploited the fact that it had been chosen by the Emperor Napoleon III as his 'Purveyor' of brandy. Although the Emperor fell from power within two years of their appointment the firm successfully fudged the distinction between Napoleon Bonaparte and his nephew by proclaiming that theirs was 'The Brandy of Napoleon'.

Courvoisier never had vineyards of its own and until recently its brandies were unremarkable, if agreeably rich. Today they are much more interesting, and the bottles, especially of the more expensive brandies, are among the most satisfying in the region. The staple VS, mostly from the Fins Bois, retains its historic character. There are two VSOPs, an ordinary Fine Champagne, and the much more interesting Millennium,

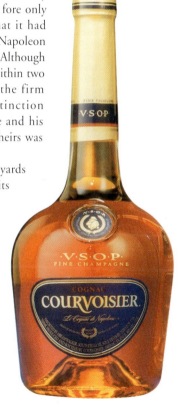

FRENCH BRANDIES

launched in 1997, which comes largely from the Borderies. The XO Imperial is elegant while the truly exquisite and well-balanced top-of-the-range Initiale Extra deservedly won the Cognac Trophy at the 1999 International Spirits Challenge.

CROIZET

The old-established family firm of Croizet has some nice standard brandies, notably the VSOP with a light floral nose, but the firm's pride and joy are its older brandies going back to the early years of the 20th century and including a classic from the 1963 vintage.

DAVIDOFF

Brand created specifically to accompany the cigars of the same name. They are naturally rich and full enough to cope with the cigars they accompany, but all are surprisingly well balanced.

Opposite
Courvoisier's headquarters on the banks of the Charente in Jarnac are a model of the triumphalism inevitable as sales soared in the third quarter of the 19th century.

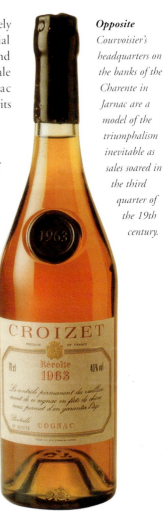

CLASSIC BRANDY

DELAMAIN

Delamain is unique, not only for the gentle style of its brandies, but also for the individuality obvious throughout the whole firm. The firm was founded in 1762 by James Delamain, from a family that had moved between Britain, Ireland and the Cognac region for over a century. James went into partnership with his father-in-law, Isaac Ranson, head of an already established firm – a frequent phenomenon in the history of Cognac. Though Bollinger now has a stake, the firm is still in the hands of the family – which includes the Braastads, Norwegians prominent in the whole region.

Delamain buys only older brandies which have been aged in old oak, and then only from a handful of suppliers in the Grande Champagne. The result is brandies which are invariably expensive but

FRENCH BRANDIES

deep, elegant and yet light. The range starts with the classic Pale & Dry, most elegant of all basic cognacs, and moves upwards through the older, more vigorous Vesper, to the unique age and delicacy of the Tres Vénérable and the summum, the Reserve de la Famille, which contains some of the oldest cognacs on the market.

JACQUES DENIS

For the past few years M Denis has been selling some of his own cognacs from the Grande Champagne. The best is the Vieille Reserve, at 44 per cent pretty hefty in theory but in reality very elegant with lots of finesse.

CLASSIC BRANDY

AE DOR

Jacques Riviere's cellar is one of the great Aladdin's caves in the Cognac region. From the – genuinely – dusty piles of bonbonnes he bottles 11 different ages, going back to some time in the early 19th century. Because they are kept in glass they display none of the signs of woodiness found in many older cognacs.

FRENCH BRANDIES

DUBOIGALANT

One of the most serious small distillers, based in the heart of the Grande Champagne. Owned by the Trijol family since 1859 it now offers three cognacs, all high quality. The VSOP is relatively old, the XO 'characteristic of eaux-de-vie more than 30 years old' while the GC Très Rare is properly full of *rancio*.

PIERRE FERRAND

M Ferrand was, indeed still is, a stern traditionalist as befits a 12th generation distiller in the heart of the Grande Champagne, who believed that cognac needs twelve years in cask before being drinkable. His passion for age – and for purity (he uses neither sugar nor caramel) gave him a deserved cult reputation. After a disagreement, his name is now used by two entrepreneurs, who keep up his traditions. The Selection des Anges was silver medalist at the 1999 International Spirit Challenge.

CLASSIC BRANDY

JEAN FILLIOUX

Founded in 1880 by a relation of the Fillioux family which has blended cognacs for Hennessy for seven generations. All the brandies come from the Grande Champagne so the best are inevitably the older brandies, the Cep d'Or (12–13 years old), the Très Vieux (20+) and the luscious Reserve Familiale (over 50 years old).

FRAPIN

This historic firm has its headquarters behind a rose-covered courtyard in Segonzac, the capital of the Grande Champagne. It is still owned by the descendants of the Frapin family, who've been around the region since the 16th century and own the biggest vineyard in the Grande Champagne, 300 hectares next to the Ragnaud-Sabourins [qv] on the chalkiest slopes in the whole Cognac region. As always with brandies made exclusively from the Grande Champagne, it is best to stick to the – very distinguished – older brandies. In 1998 the cognac named after the family estate, Chateau de Fontpinot, won the trophy for best cognac at the

FRENCH BRANDIES

ISC. Like many of the best cognacs it is not excessively old (35 years possibly) but already rounded while retaining the fruit too often lost in older brandies – though Frapin's venerable Extra Grande Champagne has a lot of fruity *rancio*.

A DE FUSSIGNY

A courageous venture by Alain Royer, of the Royer family [qv]. For over fifteen years he has been buying single lots, often a single cask, of distinguished brandies. Their quality depends on M Royer's palate which will not let you down if you are looking for a characterful individual example of an older brandy from the Grande Champagne. He also now sells a – reputable – XO.

CLASSIC BRANDY

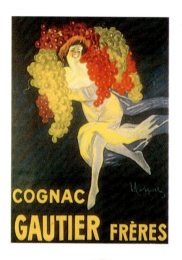

GAUTIER

The best-known brand in the Gemaco group. The finest brandy is the Pinar del Rio, smooth as befits brandy matured in ideal damp conditions (by a former water mill).

Also, fashionably, offers a cigar blend.

FRENCH BRANDIES

JULES GAUTRET

This marque can rely on the many different cognacs from the members of the Unicognac co-operative and the choice is good. Even the (four-year-old) VS is well balanced and the XO is rich and round with some *rancio*.

CLASSIC BRANDY

GODET

One of the few remaining traditional family-owned firms left in the Cognac region and one of the oldest. Indeed the reason why its offices are in the seaside town of La Rochelle, well away from Cognac, is that it was founded – in 1550 – by Bonaventure Godet, a Dutch merchant at a time when the Dutch dominated the trade in wine and *brandewijn* and operated from La Rochelle rather than from inland towns.

Today Jean-Jacques Godet and his brother, Jean-Marie, both direct descendants of Bonaventure, run a firm which offers an enterprising selection of cognacs, not only the inevitable Napoleon but also other, more delicate, blends like Excellence which incorporate brandies from the Fins Bois and from the Borderies – they even have a pure Vieilles Borderies.

86

FRENCH BRANDIES

LEOPOLD GOURMEL

One of the few new ventures in Cognac and one of the few selling almost exclusively brandies from the Fins Bois. Founded in the 1970s by Pierre Voisin, a Fiat agent with a passion for cognac. Range of cognacs from the young Age du Fruit, designed as a mixer (and, or so claims the managing director Olivier Blanc, to go with foie gras!), to the properly floral Age des Fleurs, the (spicier) Age des Epices – one of my favourite sipping cognacs – and the rather too expensive Quintessence. All come from a single vintage, all show the lightness associated with the best of the Fins Bois. Gourmel also sells a couple of astonishing single-vintage cognacs from the 1960s.

Opposite
The handsome 18th century headquarters of the family firm of Godet in La Rochelle, an accurate symbol of the firm's long history.

CLASSIC BRANDY

GOURRY DE CHADEVILLE
The Domaine de Chadeville is one of the oldest estates in the Grande Champagne. Not afraid to give precise ages to their excellent range (VSOP 8 years, Très Vieux 25, XO 35 – a golden oldie);

A HARDY
A sad story. An old-established and well-respected family firm which fell victim to the collapse of the cognac market in the late 1990s and which had to go into receivership in 1998 though it has since been bought up and remains in business. Makes some attractive products (including a delightfully elegant 20cl Fisherman's Flask to keep out the cold on the river bank). The XO is decently rounded but ends slightly thin and spirity.

FRENCH BRANDIES

JAS HENNESSY

The dominant force in the cognac business, with a steadily increasing market share, especially in the United States. Founded in 1765 by an émigré Irish army officer, James Hennessy. Until 1998 it was run by a descendant of the founder–although it had merged with Moet & Chandon in 1972 and is now part of the enormous French drink and luxury goods group LVMH-Moet Hennessy. Not surprisingly the firm had a decidedly aristocratic attitude to the business (for instance they invented but never registered the idea of putting XXX on brandy), never making much effort on the competitive French market and relying on what is now seven generations of the Fillioux family to supervise the production and blending of the firm's products. For 30 years until the late 1940s Hennessy formed a duopoly with Martell, cognac's other dominant force. They divided the world, leaving Hennessy with historically strong positions in the United States and, obviously, in Ireland, where Hennessy is virtually synonymous with cognac.

Above
James Hennessy, the Irish-born former officer of Louis XV and founder of a firm that has remained as aristocratic as he looks.

89

CLASSIC BRANDY

Opposite
Hennessy only owns a few vineyards, mostly in choice spots in the Grande Champagne.

All Hennessy's cognacs share a naturally rich, if fortunately rather dry style without any caramel overtones. Typically the XO is rich and grapey while the rich candied fruitiness of the Paradis is a model of what upper-class cognacs ought to be. The Richard is expensive (well over $1000 even in duty-free) but the money is well spent, as it's the longest cognac I've ever tasted with great warmth, balance and finesse. Once scornful of new ideas, like single-estate cognacs, or indeed of cognac as a long drink, Hennessy is now trying to update itself with a trendy website for clubbers, and even a mixing cognac, Pure White, perhaps not the most tactful name for a firm which depends so heavily on the African-American market.

French Brandies

Classic Brandy

Hine

In 1791 a young immigrant from Dorset, Thomas Hine, met a M Hennessy while imprisoned in the Chateau de Jarnac. Thus well introduced into the world of cognac he went on to marry a Mlle Delamain and to found one of the most distinguished firms in the business. Its brandies have always been exceptionally full, elegant and well balanced, neither as 'Pale & Dry' as those of their neighbours in Jarnac, the Delamains, nor as rich as those of Hennessy, now their owners. They are perhaps best known in Britain for the brandies they sent as youngsters to be matured near the docks in London and Bristol, but these are not as full or satisfying as the vintages matured nearer home. Of the non-vintage cognacs the Rare & Delicate is just what the name implies, while the Antique is a very distinguished brandy indeed, with good colour balance and elegance and the 'young adult' nose of a brandy in which the *rancio* is just developing.

FRENCH BRANDIES

LARSEN
Formerly specialists in selling to the monopoly importers in Scandinavian countries now broadening their range, mostly in fancy bottles for the Far Eastern and duty free market.

LHERAUD
One of the pioneers among growers selling their brandies directly. The Lheraud family has been distilling brandies from the wines from their 35-hectare estate in some of the best area of the Petite Champagne near Angeac since 1875. Nevertheless they started selling to the public only in 1971. Their relatively wide range of brandies from the Fins Bois as well as their own estate includes a number of most interesting single-vintage brandies, from the Grande Champagne as well as from their two home regions. Everything from the VSOP up is worth a look, though the XO is a bit young and spirity.

CLASSIC BRANDY

Opposite
For a long time Martell's Cordon Bleu, which includes a lot of brandies from the Borderies, was deservedly the only big-selling quality cognac on the market.

MARTELL

With Hennessy, historically one of the two dominant forces in the cognac business. Founded in 1715 by Jean Martell, a smuggler from the Channel Islands who greatly helped his fortunes through successive marriages to widows of the owners of two of the leading Cognac families. Unlike the dashing Hennessys, the Martells had a reputation for being down-to-earth salesmen. Part of their success was due to the style of their cognacs, which owed little or nothing to brandies from the Champagnes. They also went in for a relatively neutral, dry brandy relying on the influence of the wood to provide the necessary extra dimension to the cognac. Their best brandy, Cordon Bleu, which dominated the top end of the market until the Hennessys introduced the XO, was and remains firmly based on the nutty cognacs from the Borderies. Always deep in colour, but in danger of losing its fruit, yet it remains a model of its type.

In 1986 the Martell family finally succumbed to a ludicrously high bid from the Canadian giant Seagram which since then has tried to justify the purchase by introducing a large number of new brandies. Today Martell's offerings range from the VS up to Extra. The Cordon Bleu remains a

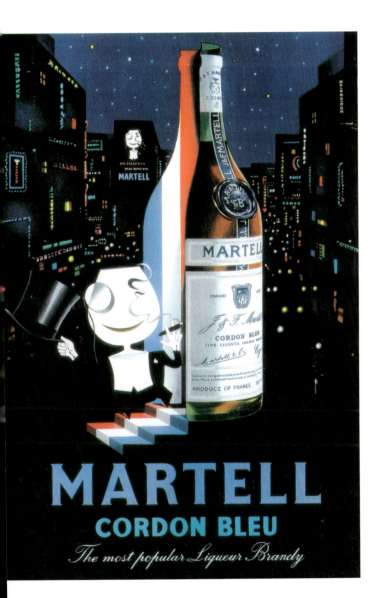

CLASSIC BRANDY

mainstay but has been joined by an XO introduced as recently as 1987, the Noblige introduced in 1994 to provide a lighter style, a Napoleon Special Reserve introduced in 1990, l'Or first sold in 1992 and – for duty free, Artys and Odys. But all share one important Martell tradition – none are either Grande or Petite Champagne.

MOYET

Until the late 1970s this was a relatively routine family firm. Then it was bought by a couple of outsiders who realised that the family's stocks were priceless, and they became known as 'the Antiquaries of Cognac'. The stocks have been refreshed with brandies that are unusually rich and young for their age, thus retaining the family style.

NORMANDIN-MERCIER

Family firm founded in 1872 by a M Jules Normandin, great-grandfather of the present owner, Jean-Marie Normandin. Until 1978 they only supplied casks of cognac to the major companies but then started to sell direct. All their

CLASSIC BRANDY

cognacs are from the Champagnes, and all are aged in old oak produced in the most natural fashion possible without additives. They also have a range of older brandies averaging over 30 years old.

OTARD

Historically important firm founded by two growers, MM Otard and Dupuy, just before the French revolution, to market their very considerable stocks. They managed to buy the most distinguished building in Cognac, the 16th-century Château de Cognac, which dominates the first bridge over the Charente, and in the early 19th century their firm ranked with Martell and Hennessy. But more recent history has seen a constant change of owners, none of whom seem to have understood the cognac business, so Otard increasingly relies on direct sales of its relatively undistinguished cognacs from visitors to the château. Typically, one of the firm's XOs, the 55, is disappointing, dominated by the burn on the palate, though, to be fair, the XO Gold has real warmth and fruit on the nose.

PLANAT

Owned by Camus [qv] and used by their owners for their best cognacs. Purveyors of one of the nicest cognacs on the market with some real depth and fruit and old enough to have lost any young spirity feel.

French Brandies

Prince de Didonne

Château de Didonne is in the usually-derided Bons Bois at Semussac near the estuary of the Gironde. But this small firm offers an excellent, surprisingly mature VSOP, and a light, well-rounded XO.

Raymond Ragnaud

Though his cognacs are not as distinguished as those from his relatives and neighbours, the Ragnaud-Sabourins, M Ragnaud's brandies do provide the drinker with a clear idea of why the slopes above Ambleville in the heart of the Grande Champagne remain the heart of the region.

Ragnaud-Sabourin

For many connoissueurs, the Ragnaud-Sabourin estate, the Domaine de la Voute above Ambleville, is the Mecca of the whole region, and with good reason since the family's fruity and well-balanced brandies remain a yardstick with which to judge the best products of the Grande Champagne. Gaston Briand started to sell his brandies direct between the wars and the tradition was carried on by his daughter and son-in-law, Denis and Marcel Ragnaud, then by their

CLASSIC BRANDY

Above

The home and distillery of the Ragnaud-Sabourin family: brandy on a domestic scale.

son and now by their daughter Patricia Ragnaud-Sabourin.

The only problem with cognacs from this chalky Mecca is that they remain rather spirity until they are about 20 years old. For the next century or so they will be sublime. Start with the (roughly) 20-year-old Reserve Speciale with its buttery richness. Although the XO is rather similar to that made by lesser distillers, the 35-year-old Fontvieille proves

FRENCH BRANDIES

that cognacs do not have to be very old to be great, though it has to be said that the 45-year-old Florilège has some of the purest *rancio* I have ever come across.

RÉMY MARTIN

An extraordinary story. In 1924 André Renaud, the most brilliant entrepreneur in the history of 20th-century Cognac, bought a virtually bankrupt firm, Rèmy Martin. In the 1930s he introduced a revolutionary product, his VSOP, based solely on brandies from the Champagnes, many of them from the superb stocks accumulated by his wife's family, the Frapins. This elegant brandy remains the standard by which all other VSOPs are judged. Later he introduced the equally elegant Louis XIII in a decorative and extremely expensive Baccarat bottle. The firm survived a serious family feud involving Renaud's two sons-in-law, Max Cointreau and André Hériard-Dubreuil, a businessman almost as brilliant as Renaud. Hériard-Dubreuil masterminded the take-over of Cointreau and the purchase of a number of champagne firms,

CLASSIC BRANDY

where he displayed the originality and boldness that was his hallmark in Cognac itself. Unfortunately over-indebtedness and over-reliance on the Chinese market caused financial problems, and the sale of Krug, though the group is now recovering under Hériard-Dubreuil's daughter, Dominique.

All Rémy's brandies share a lightness and florality, combined with the depth associated with brandies distilled from wines which retain their lees. The VSOP, with all its overtones of candied fruit remains the standard by which all other VSOPs are judged. The newly-introduced 1738 Accord Royal is richer than the other brandies

in the range, probably because it is designed to be drunk with cigars. The XO Special lingers in the palate, with the same – if stronger – overtones of candied fruit as the VSOP. The Extra is over woody but the Louis XIII combines richness depth and the Rémy florality.

ROULLET
Old family company which exploits its estate near Jarnac to offer some fine brandies from this special corner of the Fins Bois. Also has some precious stocks of older cognacs.

LOUIS ROYER
Old family company in Jarnac which was sold to the Japanese giant Suntory some years ago. Cognacs better than they were under the family.

TIFFON
Founded back in 1875 by one Méderic Tiffon and now owned by the ubiquitous Braastad family. In the past their Norwegian origins helped them dominate the Scandinavian market, itself in the hands of the three state monopolies (Norway, Sweden, Finland), and they are still major wholesalers and blenders.

UNICOGNAC
Cognac's biggest co-operative, producing a range of relatively standard brandies which sell well, largely on price, in France.

CLASSIC BRANDY

ARMAGNAC

Opposite
The vineyards of the Castarède family at the Chateau de Montiban, in the heart of Gascony and the Bas Armagnac.

Armagnac comes from Gascony, that rich French province south of Bordeaux, famous as the birthplace of the Musketeers and as the home of the world's finest foie gras. As the local Gascons, never averse to blowing their own trumpet, will inevitably inform even the most casual visitor, armagnac is at once the oldest and the youngest spirit in France. Oldest because it was first distilled in the 15th century (when it was famous for the same sort of medicinal benefits now being trumpeted today), youngest because the Armagnaçais are still arguing over how to distil it. For armagnac, sometimes to an exaggerated extent, is a better reflection of French individuality at work than any other spirit. As a result it remains one of the least industrialised of spirits, the one where amateurs can most legitimately hope to find a neglected bottle which they can cherish because it offers unique qualities –

FRENCH BRANDIES

those probably not shared even by the next cask in the cellar where it was lodged. At its best armagnac offers the drinker a depth, a natural sweetness, a fullness unmatched by even the best cognacs. A typical 20-year-old armagnac has a lovely rich balance of violets and wet woodland on the palate. But alas, armagnac is underrated because far too high a proportion is sold young.

Classic Brandy

Above
The fragrant Colombard grape, just as useful for wine as for Armagnac.

Right
Armagnacs made from the incomparable floral folle blanche.

It is also a poor relation because its promotional efforts have been less successful than those of cognac. Historically this was because armagnac, unlike cognac, is not produced in a region which has lived off trade for a millennium or more, but from the depths of Gascony, 100 miles south of Bordeaux, and well away from navigable waters. Geologically it is produced on the churned-up mess of sand and clay left behind by the ebb and flow of the sea as it retreated from the foothills of the Pyrenees, at the end of the last Ice Age. The finest armagnacs are produced to the west of the region, from the edge of the pine forests of the Landes, which has an unusual soil formation known as *boulbènes*, alluvial deposits which cover a sub-soil of sand and clay.

This western section is the heart of the Bas Armagnac, whose brandies evoke associations of plums and prunes. To the east is the Ténarèze, whose soil, a mixture of chalk and clay,

produces fine floral armagnacs reminding connoisseurs irresistibly of violets. Furthest east is the Haut Armagnac, which now produces very little brandy but a great deal of wine, especially the well-known Vin du Pays des Côtes de Gascogne. For Armagnac is warmer than Cognac (although the breezes from the Bay of Biscay ensure that it is never too hot) and the grapes ripen earlier and more fully.

The grape varieties used are also different from those used in Cognac. Although the dreary Ugni Blanc, which is ubiquitous in Cognac, is also widely planted in Armagnac, the region also retains a little of the incomparable Folle Blanche and a little also of the relatively aromatic Colombard. It also grows much more of the only hybrid allowed in any wine or spirit entitled to be called Appellation d'Origine Controlée (AOC): this is the Baco 22A, half Folle Blanche, half Noah, an infamous and over-productive hybrid. It will have to be phased out by the year 2010, but in the meantime provides the older spirits with a unique combination: the florality of the Folle Blanche and the rather foxy strength of the Noah.

Until the mid-19th century armagnac was distilled in tiny pot-stills, but the locals then adapted the continuous Coffey still to their own purposes, and it is this type which has become the 'traditional' still in the region. Today armagnac is distilled, not only à la Cognaçaise,

CLASSIC BRANDY

but in a number of different traditional fashions; truly continuously, or semi-continuously, with the *secondes*, the heavier elements, returned to the still to be redistilled, or in a still with three or four plates which provides a semi-continuous flow (stopped only for the still to be emptied and cleaned). In all the stills the wine is heated to 92–93 degrees centigrade, the point at which wine of 10 per cent alcohol boils (to get a higher-strength spirit you allow a slightly cooler wine). The strength of the final spirit depends on the number of plates in the still. The maximum is 15, which will produce a spirit of 70 per cent, while the traditional still, with five plates, will produce a spirit of a mere 60 per cent alcohol.

The older stills had even fewer plates: they were also small, and rarely cleaned, and the spirit they produced was chock-a-block with congeners, especially if the wine was distilled only to 52–53 per cent alcohol. This made an enormous difference. Wine distilled to 52 per cent alcohol contains twice as much of the congener-heavy *queues* than one distilled to the average 60 per cent alcohol normal in modern stills. This represents a difference in potential richness – and potential impurities – far greater than between spirits distilled to between 60 and 70 per cent alcohol, normal in cognac pot-stills.

Old-style armagnacs needed at least ten years before they even started to be drinkable, and, in my view, are at their best after 40 years or so.

Opposite
Casks at Sempé, one of the few firms in Armagnac with serious stocks of old brandy.

Unfortunately the producers tended to keep them in cask too long and so many of the older armagnacs on the market are far too woody and have an obvious mustiness because the wood in which they were kept was dirty.

But this is not normally a problem. In fact, precisely the opposite. By a quirk of French law, armagnac can be sold even younger than cognac, from two years upwards. Yet, even when distilled in cognac-type stills it takes longer to mature than cognac. When newly distilled it is oilier and fruitier than cognac which is relatively neutral. But when armagnac is two years old and thus marketable, it is at its most brutal, the wood in which it has been lodged has had its impact but the spirit has not blended with it, although it soon gets richer.

This incomparable spirit has been hard-hit by a number of accidents in the 100 years since it shared in the Golden Age enjoyed by all French producers of wines and spirits in the middle of the 19th century. First came that universal plague, in the shape of the *phylloxera vastatrix* louse. In Armagnac the devastation was complete, the recovery minimal, and by 1937, after the worst of the slump, the region was producing a mere 22,000 hectolitres of spirit annually, a quarter of the pre-*phylloxera* level. This disaster was compounded by two false dawns after both the world wars. The recovery after World War I was pretty minimal, so the let

FRENCH BRANDIES

down was not dramatic. But the surge of sales immediately after 1945 was dramatic and short-lived because too many young armagnacs were sold in the immediate post-war years (inevitably at low prices). The result was to give armagnac a lasting reputation as a poor relation of cognac.

In the 1950s and 60s a number of cognac houses established themselves in the region, took one look at the situation and decided that the major problem lay precisely in the time it took for brandy distilled à l'Armagnaçaise to mature. So, in the early 1970s, after a struggle with the authorities, they were allowed to introduce their own pot-stills. As can be imagined, these do indeed produce a more acceptable, if rather characterless armagnac after only a few years in

Left
Filtering the newly distilled armagnac.

CLASSIC BRANDY

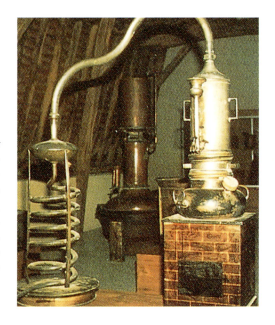

Right
A classic armagnac still at Château Maniban; note how short it is, ensuring that the brandy will be low in alcohol and therefore rich and long-lived.

wood. Now, 25 years after the first armagnacs were distilled in cognac-type stills, it is possible to agree that these do work better than the traditional type for the majority of armagnacs which are sold before their tenth birthday. But once the brandy has been in the cask for 15 years, the ability of the traditional method of distillation to extract more of the goodies from the wine show through in a richer, more complex character.

Fortunately the invasion of the Cognaçais forced the locals to improve their own stills, by trying to retain the characteristic richness of

FRENCH BRANDIES

flavour while losing some of the impurities traditionally associated with it. The experiments do not have to be on a very big scale, because most armagnacs not made by the handful of relatively sizeable firms like Janneau, Sempé and Clé des Ducs are actually distilled by a few specialists (notably M Jean-Pierre Gimet who experiments with different distillation methods) who distil on behalf of individual growers. These are far more responsible for the style of the region's brandies than are the individual proprietors who mature and sell the resulting spirit. The more reputable houses naturally mature their brandies for longer than the legal minimum, but this does not help greatly – a more rational (if inevitably less immediately profitable) policy would have been to prevent the sale of armagnacs before they were at least five years old.

In the past couple of decades the brandy's reputation has been greatly helped by the snobbery of French restaurateurs wanting to offer the single-vintage spirits not then available from Cognac. The Armagnaçais were able to offer a seemingly limitless supply of single-vintage brandies, most of which include a majority of brandies distilled within a few years of the date on the bottle – the cynicism is justified because few producers have enough casks of any particular vintage to top up the casks through the years. With the help of carbon-dating techniques the authorities are now establishing the sort of strict regulatory framework reigning in Cognac.

This is not going to help sales of armagnac which have been declining steadily over the past decade. The decline is not causing the sort of social crisis seen in Cognac because Gascony can produce so many other goodies, ranging from foie gras to some very acceptable white wines. Armagnac was never as important to the local economy as was cognac – in the 19th century they apparently distilled only when sales of wine were poor. This is fortunate for the locals, for the future seems to lie in a relatively small production of upmarket brandies from a few specialist merchants and individual estates.

FRENCH BRANDIES

ARMAGNAC – REGULATIONS AND AGES

Until 1999 the Armagnaçais followed roughly the same regulations as the Cognaçais. But they have now adopted a much simpler and more sensible classification. This, however, is only provisional since a number of merchants have objected to the elimination of such well-known (if vague) classifications as VSOP and XO.

ARMAGNAC   2 to 6 years old

VIEIL ARMAGNAC   Over 6 years old

MILLESIMES   Must be more than 10 years old

When the French authorities agree, the Armagnaçais are hoping to be allowed to sell new spirit as Blanche de l'Armagnac.

ARMAGNAC DIRECTORY

*Opposite
Gabarret, just
one of the many
picturesque small
towns in the Bas
Armagnac.*

PHILIPPE AURIAN
Founded in 1900 by a M Dupeyron, and continued by his son-in-law René Aurian. Since 1952 the Aurians have been selling armagnacs under their own name. The family own a small estate of their own but also buy in brandies. They are one of the few merchants specialising in brandies from the Ténarèze.

BARON DE SIGOGNAC
The marque belongs to a firm called Adex which owns the biggest stock of armagnacs in the region and can thus offer some extraordinary older brandies. The 20-year-old is nicely elegant but without the concentration of a great brandy. By contrast the 1961 – and the older single vintages – have a splendid truffly richness and a nose full of vanilla and caramel. As if to prove the authorities wrong in banning the Baco grape, it reinforces the richness of these brandies without any sign of the foxiness generally associated with the variety.

CASTARÈDE
The Castarède family was encouraged to set up in business as the first official merchant in Armagnac by a family friend, one M Haussmann, who went on to rebuild Paris in the mid-19th century. Today they are one of the few firms offering a serious range of armagnacs from the family estate of

BAS ARMAGNAC

i GABARRET

Classic Brandy

Right
Château de Maniban, historically the covetable home of the Castarède family.

Maniban, real, chewy, rich armagnacs; stuff designed for the amateur and not for the faint-hearted.

French Brandies

Château de Cassaigne

The Faget family have owned this picturesque house and its 27 hectares of vines for seven generations. The armagnacs are better than average and the château is open to visitors and well worth a visit.

Château Laballe

Noël Laudet, descendant of the ship owner who bought the estate back in 1820, is a distinguished former director of Château Beychevelle in the Medoc. The brandies from the family estate are kept in new wood and so need a long time to mature, but they are well worth waiting for.

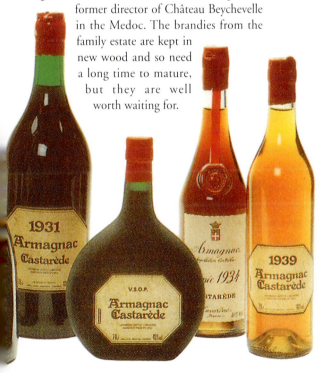

Château de Lacaze

A fine estate planted with suitable grape varieties, centred on a medieval Château – what could go wrong? Well, a lot actually. In the early 1980s it was owned by an English entrepreneur, Christopher Oldham, who had the bright idea of selling casks of newly distilled brandy to English buyers, mostly in the City of London. Then he sold the estate to a Japanese lady who turned out to be a major fraudster. The brandies were rescued and are now lodged in suitable British cellars. They are excellent examples of traditional armagnacs and very good value.

Château de Laubade

In 1974 this estate, the largest in the Armagnac region, was bought by a seed merchant, M Jean-Jacques Lesgourgues, who pioneered the sale of armagnacs from a single estate. M Lesgourgues offers traditionally distilled armagnacs which he keeps for three years in new oak. His range starts at VSOP, because he is interested only in selling older brandies, and goes back to a 1935 vintage brandy.

Château de Tariquet

This is a big family-owned estate in the heart of the Bas Armagnac which has expanded rapidly since the 1960s. While best known for its wines sold as Vins de Pays de Gascogne, the owners, the Grassa family, also offer a number of very carefully

FRENCH BRANDIES

made brandies. Unusually – possibly uniquely – it sells a range of armagnacs from four to twelve years old made purely from the Folle Blanche which show this variety in all its floral glory. But its more orthodox brandies are also worth looking at – especially the fruity rich VSOP – while it also sells a properly tarry 1972 vintage at its natural strength of 45 per cent alcohol.

CLASSIC BRANDY

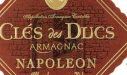

CLEF DES DUCS

The armagnac subsidiary of the Rémy-Cointreau empire which has ensured that the firm's relatively ordinary products, mostly too young for comfort, get wide distribution.

LA CROIX DE SALLES

Old-established and well-respected firm owned by the Dartigalongue family. Although they use cognac-type stills for their younger brandies, their best offerings are made traditionally from the grapes from their estate in the heart of the Bas Armagnac.

ANDRÉ DAGUIN

The high priest of the local gastronomic scene. He hunts out small lots of brandies of every age from selected growers in every part of the region including, unfashionably, the Haut Armagnac.

FRANCIS DARROZE

The son of a famous restaurateur, M Darroze does not sell brandies under his own name, but only of

FRENCH BRANDIES

the estates from which he buys his armagnacs. He is seemingly engaged in a perpetual truffle-hunt, sniffing out small distillers with stocks of old brandies. He ensures that they keep them in clean old wood in two different cellars, one damper than the other, to control the speed of maturation. He then sells small lots from individual casks. Not surprisingly he has the best range of single-vintage, characterful brandies in the region.

DOMAINE DE BOINGNÈRES

A truly classic armagnac estate situated in the sandy wastes of the Grand Bas. It has been family-owned since 1807 and was publicised between the wars by Raymond Baudoin, founder of the magazine *Revue du Vin de France*. It is now owned and managed by the formidable Madame Martine Lafitte, a descendant of the M Boingnères who gave his name to the estate. The brandy is

based on the Folle Blanche variety with some Colombard and Ugni Blanc, but kept to low yields – a mere ten hectolitres of spirit for every hectare of vines. The wine is distilled only to 52 per cent alcohol and the young spirit is kept in new oak for two years. The result is a truly traditional

CLASSIC BRANDY

armagnac full of warmth and bite. Vintages like the 1965 and even the still-a-little young 1979 have won the trophy for best armagnac at the International Spirits Challenge whenever they were entered.

Opposite
A delightful ad for one of Gélas' cognacs no longer produced.

GÉLAS

A most reliable and well-established family firm, distilling their brandies in two ancient stills, on their lees, to the traditional strength, and keeping them in new wood until they are bottled. The company used to sell a wide variety of single-vintage brandies.

FRENCH BRANDIES

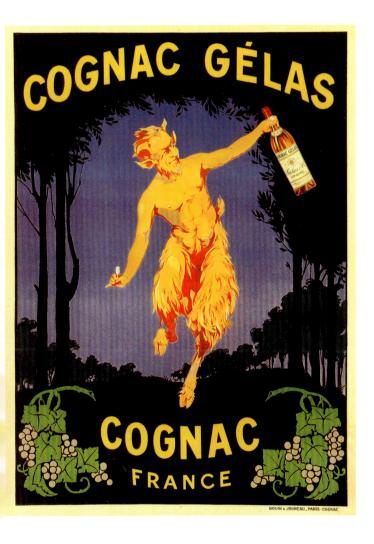

JANNEAU

Still the leading firm in Armagnac despite a chequered recent history. In 1988 it was sold by the Janneau family to Seagram-Martell who neglected it. Five years later it was resold to Antonio Giovanetti, who had made a fortune selling single malt whiskies in Italy. After a period of hesitation it is now being run by Willy Phillips, who made the name of Macallan single malt whisky and thus well understands the blending of fine spirits. Thanks to his know-how and the firm's very considerable stocks of older brandies Janneau now has the best range of standard armagnacs on the market. Even the VS is light and floral. The XO is rather spirity but has a delightful, pruny, nutty flavour. And the Grande Fine Armagnac is for me the finest blend on the market. Made from spirits between 15 and over 30 years old it's got a lot of *rancio*; it's rich, it's earthy, and yet retains some elegance.

LABERDOLIVE

Gerald Laberdolive's father was one of the pioneers in selling single-estate, single-vintage armagnacs and the son is continuing the good work. You may be sure that all the family's single-domaine brandies, d'Escoubes, de Jaurey, de Pillon and de Labrune will be of the age they claim, and show

FRENCH BRANDIES

the best of the character of that particular vintage – no ordinary claim.

LARRESINGLE

The Etablissements Papelorey, makers of Larresingle, were founded way back in 1837 – probably the first specialist merchant in the region – by the splendidly named Hippolyte Pappelorey. His descendants were the first merchants to bottle all their brandies before selling them; a major step forward in retaining control over their quality. Today the fifth generation of the family continues the family tradition and all their brandies above the rather basic XXX are sound stuff. Unusually they even sell a pure and very typical brandy made solely from wines from the Ténarèze.

DE MAILLAC

The chateau dates back to the 12th century – which counts as old even in Armagnac – and was bought by the Bertholon family in the early 20th century. The Bertholons are firm traditionalists, selling only older brandies which they buy in with considerable care. They introduced the label Hors d'Age to indicate brandies aged between 10 and 20 years old. Their finest offering is a pure Folle Blanche which shows what was lost with the virtual abandonment of this uniquely fragrant variety.

CLASSIC BRANDY

MARQUIS DE MONTESQUIOU

This classic armagnac estate of 90 hectares, dating back to the 11th century, is now owned by French spirits giant Pernod-Ricard. They produce relatively standard armagnacs, none of any great age, as well as a few single vintages which are well worth tasting.

DE MONTAL

This is a sound business established at yet another of the region's historic houses, the Château Le Rieutort, and has been family-owned for three centuries. The company specialises in blends based on stocks drawn from local co-operatives.

RYST-DUPEYRON

M Jacques Ryst, whose family firm was founded in 1905, is a traditionalist and so are his armagnacs (and none the worse for that). Even the XO is at least ten years old and it, like the older brandies, is made in traditional continuous stills.

FRENCH BRANDIES

SAMALENS

This family-owned business was founded in 1882 by the great-grandfather of the present owners, Pierre and Philippe Samalens. They use only wine from the Bas Armagnac distilled in old stills to a relatively low strength, then age the brandy for the first two years in small casks of the dark local oak under the eaves of their cellar. This concentrates the spirit, but means that it needs longer to soften, because the sojourn leaves a bourbon feel – of burnt fruit. Yet even the VSOP offers a

CLASSIC BRANDY

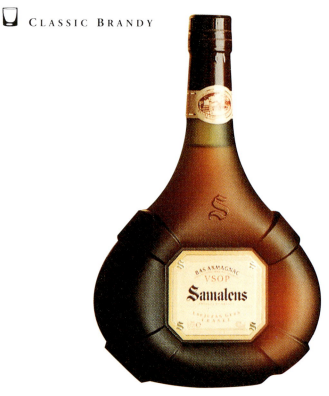

nice compromise, the fruitiness and slight brutality of the classic armagnac is softened by the spirit made in cognac stills. Their Vieille Relique is both deep and profoundly satisfying.

SEMPÉ

Founded in 1934 by a local legend, Henri-Abel Sempé, who started bottling at the age of 16 before going on to become a senator for the region. Its standard blends are relatively ordinary but its more mature and single-vintage brandies

FRENCH BRANDIES

are anything but. The 15-year-old has a delightful, light, almondy nose, and is relatively young and sprightly. The 1963 proved a winner at the International Spirits Challenge, as a classic, traditional, rich armagnac, while the 1965 has all the roundness, the warmth, the fruity-nutty-cake feel of a very fine brandy indeed – and, moreover, you would never guess that it weighed in at 47 per cent alcohol.

CLASSIC BRANDY

OTHER FRENCH BRANDIES

An unhappily growing number of French brandies consist merely of neutral alcohol flavoured with strongly-flavoured *eaux de vie*. But the real stuff, mostly in the form of marc, is available from a wide variety of sources. None of them make enough spirit to justify a separate entry but you can be sure that winemakers as reputable as those of Louis Latour in Burgundy or Château Grillet on the Rhône are not going to risk their reputation by marketing a spirit unworthy of their standing – so rely on the name on the bottle.

There are a great many producers and none of them make brandies in any great quantity. This is because traditionally thrifty peasants in every grape-growing French province refused to waste their lees, or wine too sour to be drinkable; they made it into marc, or brandy, which the Burgundians still call *fine*.

In Burgundy there are two factories distilling the lees as well as a number of mobile stills, and a handful of estates and firms proudly offer their own oak-aged marcs. These are aromatic, rich, and powerful – many of them are sold at a daunting strength of 45 per cent alcohol or more. Such brandies are the ideal conclusion to a gigantic Burgundian repast for gourmands not overly interested in extending their life-span. Perhaps inevitably the Burgundians have their own method of distillation; the marcs – which they call *gennes* –

FRENCH BRANDIES

and the wines are distilled slowly, often without their stalks, as *marc égrappé*. The best marcs are those which have been aged for up to ten years in the oak barrels previously used to age the wine.

In Champagne virtually all the *marc de champagne* is distilled at the Distillerie Goyard at Ay which buys all the surplus lees from the Champagne region. In a unique distillation system known as *en calandre* the wines are first heated by steam in three interconnected vessels each holding about 400 litres. The fumes they give off, which are about 20 per cent alcohol, are then distilled to about 70 per cent. The only other French region offering marcs in any quantity is Alsace, home of many fine brandies made from other fruits, and where the co-operatives have a long tradition of making brandies from the local grapes, most notably the floral *Gewürtstraminer*. Home-aged marcs are also a by-product in other winemaking regions, notably the Jura (where they also make brandy) and Provence.

Above
A splendidly ripe bunch of the Gewürtztraminer grapes which the Alsatians transform into fragrant marcs.

CLASSIC BRANDY

SPANISH BRANDIES

Spanish brandy has a longer history than cognac; it's more varied and in some ways more intriguing. Most of the brandies should be called Brandy de Jerez because they are distilled and sold by the firms that make sherry. Brandy-making in Spain goes back to the early Middle Ages when the Moors occupied southern Spain, and Jerez, as its full name 'de la Fontera' suggests, was on the frontier between Christendom and the then more civilised Moorish Kingdom of Granada.

The brandy-making tradition disappeared until the arrival of the Dutch in the late 17th century, looking for brandy for their sailors as they had earlier in Cognac. The locals then developed what they called *holandas*, still the name used in Jerez for brandy distilled to the same 70 per cent alcohol level as cognac. The next impetus came when Cognac was invaded by the *phylloxera vastatrix* louse in the late 19th century and Brandy de Jerez filled the gap for a couple of decades until Jerez too was hit by the bug. But the real boom was triggered by the

Opposite
The cellars of Sanchez Romate, producers of one of Jerez' most remarkable brandies, Cardenal Mendoza.

demand from soldiers on both sides in the Spanish Civil War in the late 1930s. Spain's post-war industrialisation then carried on the good work by creating a demand from industrial workers looking for inner warmth and from better-heeled customers wanting a more civilised spirit. Until habits started to change – and duties soared – in the 1980s, brandy-making kept many famous sherry producers afloat during decades when that drink became cheap and unfashionable.

Recently domestic demand has dropped substantially. This is partly the result of tax increases – including a very sudden and substantial one in July 1996 – but is also due to a generational shift as older drinkers have died off and the basic demand from industrial workers has dampened down as the need for manual labour in industry gradually disappeared. The Jerezanos are making efforts (more intelligent than their brandy-brothers in Cognac) to attract younger drinkers with the idea that their brandy is suitable as a long drink – which of course it is, being richer and thus better able to act as a mixer than cognac. The Jerezanos have also increased their exports, not only to Spanish-speaking countries in Latin America (and to the Philippines) but also to markets like Gemany which appreciate their rich style.

The Jerezanos met the demand unleashed by the post-war boom, not by using their own

SPANISH BRANDIES

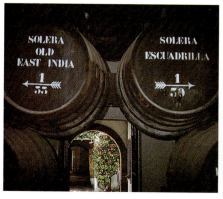

precious Palamino grapes but by going north to La Mancha, the enormous, arid plain south of Madrid dedicated to the characterless Airen grape. The wine and the brandy distilled at the nearby town of Tomelloso were both cheap. But the grapes are too rich – picked at between 11 and 13 per cent alcohol compared with the 8–9 usual in Cognac – and do not have the crisp acidity found in the Ugni Blanc grapes used in cognac. So they can never produce truly complex, great brandies however long they are matured.

Above
The venerable bodegas of Lustau, better known for their excellent range of sherries.

The Spanish produce a variety of raw spirits. A few are single- or double-distilled in the pot-stills used for cognac imitations in the late 19th century. But the vast majority of the spirit is distilled continuously, albeit to three very different strengths. Apart from *holandas*, there's

CLASSIC BRANDY

aguardiente, of between 70 and 80 per cent alcohol, and *destilado* of up to 95 per cent. But even at this high strength there's some aromatic richness in the newly-distilled spirit, even though none of the firms use it for their finest products, and under EU regulations, only half of even the most ordinary brandy can be made from *destilado*.

The raw spirit is then brought to Jerez where, following the tradition established for producing sherry, it is matured in *soleras*, three-high tiers of casks, using barrels which have held sherry for at least three years. What the Jerezanos call 'dynamic' maturation (as opposed to 'static' ageing when brandy is simply left to sleep in its wooden coffins) greatly speeds the maturation process, especially as the spirit is usually moved three or four times a year between levels of the *solera*. As a result basic brandy can be sold after only six months in cask, a sixth of the minimum required

Right
The solera system, with the casks piled three high in the cellar, is fundamental to the production of sherry – and of Brandy de Jerez.

SOLERA
DOMECQ
ARLOS I.

CLASSIC BRANDY

in Cognac, the second grade Reserva at a mere year and even the top grade, Gran Reserva, after only three years. In fact most reputable firms keep brandies in cask much longer.

Variety and warmth are the two key words to have in mind when assessing Brandies de Jerez. The warmth comes partly through the use of additives, including prunes and prune extract, almonds and other fruit and nuts, partly because the casks are already impregnated with sherry. Moreover, and this is the fun of Spanish brandy, styles vary enormously, partly because of the types of cask used, more because of house traditions. Brandies matured in casks which had contained Oloroso will inevitably produce richer brandies – the most extreme example being Cardenal Mendoza, the Gran Reserva made by Sanchez Romate, and the favourite of Hispanic connoisseurs the world over.

Ever since it first appeared over the English drinker's horizon 30 or 40 years ago Spanish brandy has had a – largely unjustified – bad name. It wasn't noble or historic, it wasn't called cognac or armagnac, and, what's more, it was Spanish, and thus associated with drunken nights in bars in downmarket Spanish holiday resorts. The only name that swam into the drinker's consciousness was 'Fundador' a brand name which, like Hoover or Biro, came to cover the whole gamut; although Fundador, made by Domecq, was and remains the archetype of the

Spanish Brandies

best sort of Spanish brandy, warm and rich without being cloying.

Not surprisingly, it is the Gran Reservas which offer greater complexity, greater strength (40 per cent alcohol as against 36–37 per cent for the cheaper brandies) and even greater variety since each firm can afford to flaunt its particular qualities. The firms' top brandies tend to be a celebration of the glory days of Spain in the late 16th and 17th centuries. Gonzalez Byass' Lepanto is named after the great sea battle that rid the Mediterranean of the Turks in 1571, Bobadilla's Gran Capitan is named after Pissarro, conqueror of Peru, Sanchez Romate's Cardenal Mendoza celebrates the warlike prelate who headed the army that finally drove the Moors from Spain, while the Gran Duque d'Alba is named after the viceroy whose cruelties drove the inhabitants of what is now the Netherlands to revolt and establish an independent Dutch state.

CLASSIC BRANDY

BRANDIES DE JEREZ – DIRECTORY

BOBADILLA

This well-regarded firm is now owned by Osborne, but run as a separate entity. The 103 brand is light and appreciated mainly in Spain although Bobadilla's relatively dry 103 Etiqueta Bianco would be fine with ginger ale.

LUIS CABALLERO

This family firm made its name from the surprisingly delicious Ponche liqueur and bought up Lustau with the profits. Caballero's own Milenario is properly rich on the nose while the palate brings out a delicious blend of plums and blackberries.

DOMECQ

A family firm famous for its sherries, and pioneer of Spanish brandy, Domecq's origins date back to the 18th century. But its rise to fame and fortune started in the early 19th century when the firm of Ruskin, Telford and Domecq dominated the British trade in sherry (though Ruskin's son John preferred to write on art and architecture).

In 1869 Juan Pedro Domecq, then head of the firm, died childless and left the firm to his adopted son, also called Juan Pedro. A

Spanish Brandies

relative, Pedro Domecq Lustau, who was born near Cognac, was responsible for pioneering the sale of Brandy de Jerez. The family had been distilling it in small quantities for some time but it was Pedro Domecq who launched the Fundador brand in 1874, five years before the arrival of the *phylloxera* louse in the Charentes interrupted the supply of cognac and gave the Jerezanos a chance to supply world markets with brandy. Until recently Fundador was the biggest single brand of Spanish brandy.

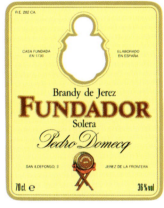

The Domecqs also pioneered the production of Spanish-style brandy in Mexico but they sold out to the British group Allied-Domecq in the early 1990s. Today they still offer the best range of standard Brandies de Jerez, all sharing the Jerez qualities of warmth and character. For a long time the name of their basic brand, Fundador, was synonymous with Spanish brandy in Britain and rightly so, for Fundador is a refined brandy with some plummy richness because half, an unusually high proportion, consists of *holandas*. Of their better qualities, Carlos III and above all their Gran Reserva Carlos I remain long and – unusually for such brandies – remarkably clean.

CLASSIC BRANDY

GARVEY

Founded way back in 1780 by an Irish immigrant, William Garvey Power. Recently the firm has passed through a number of hands. Its basic Esplendido brand is rich, unremarkable and relatively successful – in Spain at least. Its better brandies (Gran Garvey and Renacimento) are drier, more delicate and interesting, but, alas, less commercially successful.

GONZALEZ BYASS

Right
These pot-stills at Gonzalez Byass date back to the late 19th century, when Jerez temporarily took over brandy production from Cognac.

This family firm – the largest and one of the best-respected in Jerez – started distilling wine only three years after it was founded in 1835. Fifty years later they started using pot-stills to produce brandy to replace the supplies of cognac devastated by *phylloxera*. At that point they started the *solera* which produces Lepanto, their Gran Reserva, which remains the most elegant and delicate of all the Brandies de Jerez, the only one comparable with a VSOP cognac, rich and pure with lovely baked apple notes on the nose. In the 1960s, Soberano – with its excellent

Spanish Brandies

overtones of distilled sultanas – became and remained the biggest seller among the basic brandies.

CLASSIC BRANDY

GRAN DUQUE D'ALBA

A rich, unremarkable Gran Reserva originally blended by Luis Mateos, the evil genius of Jerez who brought down the price (and quality) of the region's sherries.

EMILIO LUSTAU

Lustau started as an *almacanista* or wholesaler of sherries but has emerged over the past 20 years as possessing the single best range of sherries. It is now owned by Luis Caballero [qv] which, happily,

Spanish Brandies

is encouraging the firm to remain devoted to quality. Not surprisingly, Lustau offers four fine brandies; the basic Decano is straight and correct, and the Solera Reserva is relatively unremarkable, but the Millenario Gran Reserva is rich and creamy and the Señor Lustau has a superb chocolate cream feel both on nose and palate, as well as a finish of prunes and demerara sugar. A more complex brandy than most of its competitors, it retains the delicate floral nose of a young cognac.

Osborne

This family-owned firm (pronounced Osbornay) is the biggest supplier of Brandies de Jerez since it has clearly developed a formula for producing rich brandies. Its basic Veterano, like its other brandies, is enriched by a secret mixture including prunes and nuts. Its Reserva, Magno, is a best-seller in Spain, not surprisingly since it is unusually fresh, combining the richness of distilled plum jam with overtones of nut kernels. Its Independencia is rich, showing

that it contains lots of pruny extract. But the firm's masterpiece is its most upmarket offering,

CLASSIC BRANDY

Above
Osborne bulls are landmarks throughout Spain…

Conde de Osborne. The Conde is out of this world, if only because the bottle, a duck-shaped, lop-sided fantasy, a veritable leaning bottle of Jerez, was designed by none other than Salvador Dali. It's recognisably from the same stable as Magno, with the same pruny-almondy notes on nose and palate, but with far greater refinement and delicacy.

SPANISH BRANDIES

SANCHEZ ROMATE

This small family firm is best known for its extraordinary and unique Gran Reserva, Cardenal Mendoza, named after the belligerent bishop who helped to drive the Moors from Spain. It was first produced for the family, who clearly shared the tastes of the wealthy among the Spanish-speaking population throughout the

...especially on lonely hilltops where they are favourite spots for courting couples.

CLASSIC BRANDY

world. Cardenal Mendoza is pure *holandas* and is unusually strong – it weighs in at 45 per cent alcohol. The key to its uniqueness is that it is matured in casks which have contained oloroso sherry. This shows in the style, rich, but not too heavy and without any overt spiritiness, despite its strength.

Spanish Brandies

Terry

Like Garvey, Terry was founded by an Irish immigrant. In the early 1880s it was one of the pioneers of production of Brandy de Jerez and after the war found considerable success with its Centenario which has the nut-kernel feel characteristic of all the firm's brandies. Terry's Imperio is deliberately Frenchified, like a three- to five-year-old cognac – though not as harsh. The upmarket Primero is pure *holandas*, a classic Spanish brandy, rich warm and rather bland with a decided kick in the tail.

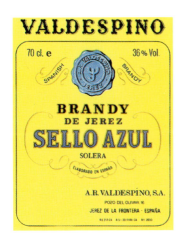

Valdespino

Until the family sold out in late 1999 Valdespino was one of the oldest family firms in the world.

Classic Brandy

The family claim descent from an ancestor who helped the King of Spain evict the Moors from Jerez in 1264, and was awarded a grant of land in recognition of his efforts. They also, or so they say, started distilling in 1500 (what is certain is that they own the oldest still in the region of Jerez). Unusually it still uses some grapes from Jerez in its blends. Today they offer two distinguished brandies, the ten-year-old Sello Azul (Blue Seal) and the older Alfonso el Sabio (named after a fabled monarch Alfonso the Wise). Both share the house style, which is full and rich – thanks to the sherry wood casks – but naturally so and unusually this owes nothing to caramel.

Spanish Brandies

Brandy de Jerez – the rules and regulations

The Jerezanos divide their newly distilled brandy into three, depending on its strength:

Holandas: below 70 per cent alcohol

Aguardiente: 70–80 per cent

Destilado de vino: 80–95 per cent

Alquitara means pot-still spirit of any strength which can be either single or double-distilled.

Ages
Brandy de Jerez: a minimum of six months in cask
Reserva: a year in cask
Gran Reserva: three years in cask – though most reputable firms only sell their brandies after a much longer period of maturation.

CLASSIC BRANDY

CATALAN BRANDY

Opposite
Torres' vineyards in the high Penedes above Barcelona are ideal for the production of sharp, acid wines suitable for brandy.

Jerez is not the only source of brandy in Spain, there are two companies in the north-eastern province of Catalonia who make their own brandies in styles totally different from those of their southern compatriots. They are lucky in that the local grape varieties, notably the Parellada, are decently acid and thus more suitable for distillation than the Airen used in Jerez, and that the Catalans are quite happy to learn from, and indeed, imitate the methods used in Cognac.

MASCARO

A most original brandy-maker, Antonio Mascaro Carbonell distils wines made from local grapes in cognac-style alembics and then ages them in Limousin oak. He offers three brandies according to their ages of which the VO is three years old or more and the Narciso at least five years old. More complex and rounded is the Don Narciso made from the acid (and therefore suitable) Pacabeo and Parellada grape varieties and aged for at least eight years. Mascaro's Estilo Fine

154

CLASSIC BRANDY

Opposite
The iron gate of the Torres distillery, emblazoned with the family's crest.

Marivaux is more delicate, with a nose like a cognac from the Fins Bois, and a palate comparable to a VSOP, with a surprisingly agreeable touch of pears in the finish. Mascaro's range is completed by a promising-sounding marc, double-distilled from the Parellada grape.

TORRES

It was natural for Catalonia's biggest and most famous producer of still wines to make a range of distinctive brandies. I found the Torres 10 Gran Reserva rather dry and woody. By contrast the higher-priced Imperial was rich, fruity and nutty as was the Fontenac, named after an old farmhouse where it's distilled and aged.

Jaime I, housed in a shell-like bottle in homage to one of Antoni Gaudi's most famous buildings in Barcelona, La Pedrera, has some old *soleras* reinforced with some younger Folle Blanche. The Jaime I, which contains some double-distilled brandy, is long, pruny and caramely – a most agreeable brandy. The Torres family also distils some marcs from their best vintages.

CLASSIC BRANDY

ITALIAN BRANDIES

BRANDY

Italian brandy has a long history – even Leonardo da Vinci sketched ideas on the subject of alembics – indeed the Italians are convinced that the word brandy is derived from the Piedmontese word *branda* which has the same meaning as *eau de vie*. Thanks to official grants and tax records we know that brandy was being produced in northern Italy as early as the late 16th century. Like the Spanish, the Italian brandy business received a considerable boost in the 1880s when the cognac merchants looked far afield to find sources of grapes and wine to replace those nearer home destroyed by the *phylloxera* bug. At that point, allegedly, Lionello Stock, the father of modern Italian brandy, exclaimed 'we could make cognac in Trieste!'

Opposite
The Trentino, the valley of the Adige, source of many of Italy's finest grappas.

Legally, Italian brandy was born in 1948 when the Italian government agreed to ban the use of the word *conac* on the bottles of Italian brandy – the decision was relatively easy given the alleged origins of the word brandy. There are two levels,

CLASSIC BRANDY

standard and de luxe categories similar to blended Scotch whisky. Brandies can be sold after two years in the wood but most standard Italian brandies have been aged for around six years, while ten is the normal age for high-end brandies. Words like Vecchio or Stravecchio or Old, XO or VSOP are purely marketing terms and do not reflect the age of the brandy. The market is dominated by two firms, Buton and Stock.

BUTON

The largest brandy firm in Italy was founded in the late 18th century by a Frenchman from the Charente, Jean Bouton, who brought with him the distilling techniques from his birthplace. Today it is controlled by the Sassolli de Bianhi family, direct descendants of the Medicis. Their Vecchia Romagna is the only Italian brandy made in traditional pot-stills. Moreover, by using the Trebbiano grape (another name for the Ugni Blanc used in cognac), by double-distilling the wine to the same strength as cognac and then maturing the brandy in old oak for at least three years Buton achieves a depth, richness and cleanliness rare among brandies made outside Cognac. They offer a number of spirits: Vecchia Romagna Etichetta Nera (minimum three years old), Oro (seven) and above all Vecchia Romagna Riserva Rare. This brandy – its constituent spirits at least 15 years old – was first marketed in 1990 to celebrate the company's 170th anniversary.

ITALIAN BRANDIES

STOCK

In 1884 young Lionello Stock saw how wines from round Trieste – then the major port in the Austro-Hungarian empire – were being shipped to Cognac, whose own vineyards had been virtually destroyed by the *phylloxera* louse. Why not, he thought, make our own cognac? So he did, until his death in 1948. He started with what he called Cognac Medicinal and in 1935 produced his 1884 Cognac Fine Champagne – a name which later had to be changed to Brandy Stock 84 but it is still the company's staple product. Lionello did not confine his efforts to Italy but expanded to produce brandies throughout central Europe and the Levant. The business was virtually destroyed in World War II but rebuilt afterwards using television advertising to particular advantage. Although Stock was acquired by the major German distiller Eckes in 1995, the brandies retain their quality level. All are single-distilled in cognac-type stills. The

CLASSIC BRANDY

Below
Ornate barrels at Stock, one of Italy's two major brandy producers.

basic brandy, the 84 VSOP, has been aged in wood for four years, it is light-orange-yellow, a nice, mature, grapey nose, some vanilla on the palate, and, like all young spirits, some fire on the finish. Its older blends, like its XO, are smooth, with some woody intensity.

ITALIAN BRANDIES

GRAPPA

A few years ago, when I was organising my first tasting of grappas, many of my friends claimed that 'there are only two types of grappa, four star and unleaded'. This was the image – and to a certain extent the reality – of the grappa scene in the early 1990s, in Britain anyway (to be fair the northern Italians and, to a certain extent, the Americans as well, were already aware of the quality of some of the better grappas). But my friends, and I must confess that I shared their reactions, were thinking of the handful of what one might call 'industrial' grappa, distilled in large continuous stills, which were the only ones available outside their native regions until comparatively recently. But now, in line with the fashion for all things Italian, connoisseurs are gradually beginning to appreciate the subtleties of the increasing number of *artisanale* grappas lovingly distilled by individuals in small, specialised stills. Unfortunately, Italians being the way they are, there are so many small distillers making tiny quantities of grappas, often delicious and sold in the most elegant of Venetian bottles, that I simply can't keep track of them all. Every half-decent Italian restaurant in London (or New York, or Chicago) seems to have its own supplier which is nice for diners but a nightmare for compilers of directories who have to confine themselves to a relative handful of producers.

CLASSIC BRANDY

ITALIAN BRANDIES

In north-eastern Italy, above all in the valley of the Adige (the Trento), in Fruili and the Veneto (Venice's hinterland), grappa started among the vineyard owners. They were almost all peasants with tiny holdings, who wrested every scrap of goodness from their precious grapes – in the same way that they used every particle of flesh and bone from their even more precious pigs. They would water the lees from the grapes and distil the resulting grape-water, what the French would call *piquette*. Unfortunately the lees had usually hung around for some weeks and had often started to re-ferment, giving the resulting spirit a decided impression of being made from silage. Nevertheless the resulting grappa, often mixed with the lees of a cup of coffee – *correto* – formed an excellent start to the working day, and it remains an incomparable cheerer-up on a dank, cold, winter morning.

But it is a long way from these peasant pick-me-ups to the fine grappas made today. First came the fiery and unremarkable grappas produced on an industrial scale by firms like Nardini. Even with these grappas the basic quality is high thanks to a decree promulgated in 1933. To ensure that it was pure, grappa had to be bottled and no longer sold in demi-johns holding 40 bottles or more. A boom in grappa consumption in the 1960s led to industrial-scale production in continuous stills and some of these

Opposite
Typically elegant grappa bottles, hand-blown for Villa de Varda, one of the most original producers in the Trentino.

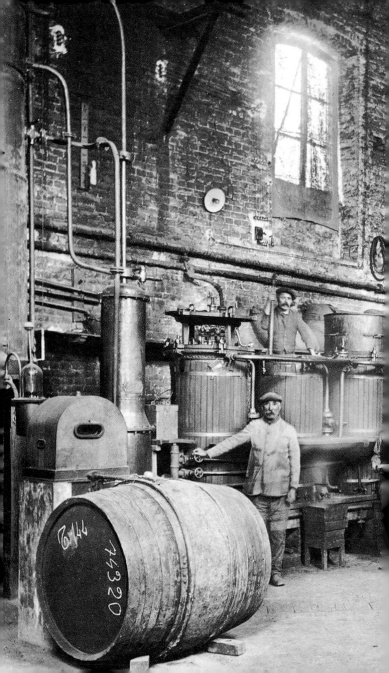

ITALIAN BRANDIES

industrial grappas are perfectly agreeable, if a little petroly, once they have been aged in wood for a year or two.

The renaissance of grappa was triggered by a pioneering distiller in Friuli, Nonino, who not only made fine grappas but also set another trend by using elegant hand-blown bottles to market his precious spirit. Today the particularly Italian nature of grappa is emphasised, not only by the elegance of the container, but also by the individuality of the distiller, each of whom uses different grape varieties – and often alters his stills to suit his own taste. But the 'new-style' grappas share one key feature: they are *monovitigno*, made from a single grape variety. By contrast industrial grappas are made from an unpredictable mix of grapes, so that the spirit does not reflect the character of a single variety. Yet for the producers the *typicité*, the closeness of the relationship of the grappa to the original grape variety is not their most important aim. They're looking

Left
Early and unusual stills at Bocchino, one of the pioneers of quality grappa.

CLASSIC BRANDY

first of all for freshness and a more general fruitiness. To retain these crucial qualities such grappas are not generally matured in wood but are stored in glass containers – not surprisingly most traditional makers don't believe that grappa improves with age since it loses its essential fruity freshness.

Above
Nonino's bottles are instantly recognisable – as are its grappas matured in small oak casks.

After distillation the grappa is chill-filtered to remove any bitterness from the pips, and is normally bottled and sold in the spring following distillation. But there is a minority which believes in ageing grappa. Certainly the Germans believe so and greatly appreciate grappas that have been aged for a couple of years in casks previously used to mature wine.

The increasing quality of the products on offer has been recognised by the International Spirits

ITALIAN BRANDIES

Challenge, with awards to grappas which were described as 'complex', intensely fruity' and 'delicate.' We're a long way from the petrol pumps here, arriving at a type of drink with, at its best, a lovely length and oiliness, comparable with many more expensive brandies and, in many cases, offering the aromas and overtones of

Below
Casks at Nardini.

CLASSIC BRANDY

Above
Old-fashioned basket press for white grapes at Bocchino.

the grape variety from which it has been distilled.

The path to better grappas was boosted by what was then called the European Community. In 1970 Brussels decided that a tenth of all the grape juice produced in the community should go for distillation, As a result the growers no longer bothered to squeeze every drop of juice from their lees before shipping it off for

ITALIAN BRANDIES

distillation, they could afford to leave a decent amount of juice in the lees and thus greatly improve the quality of the raw material used in making grappa. It helped that gentler modern presses ensured that the juice had not become overly bitter by being too harshly squeezed.

Obviously the nature of the lees – *vinaccia* is the Italian term – available depends on whether the original grapes were black or white. The black lees will contain a healthy proportion of already fermented red wine (which means that the result will be richer, nearer to brandy made from wine, than grappa made from white grapes). By contrast *vinaccia* made from white grapes will have undergone little, if any, fermentation. This in turn alters the character of the resulting grappas. Those made from red grapes are hardier, those from white grapes need very careful handling to avoid unwanted fermentation between the moment the lees are collected and the time they are distilled. For the same reason, the lees from white grapes retain more of the inherent qualities, particularly the aromas, of their original raw material, than those made from black grapes. Yet the use of white grapes poses a danger; because the raw material hasn't been fermented, there is a risk that if the juice is not distilled immediately it will turn into vinegar.

This reinforces the mantra repeated by all serious distillers which states the need to ensure that the raw material is distilled while still fresh in order to conserve all the aromas in the lees. Like the best winemakers they go on to emphasise that it is the quality of the raw material that is of primordial importance. Fortunately not all the *vinaccia* arrives at the same time, the harvest lasts a long time, enabling the distillers, working up to 18 hours a day, to work flat out for three months, completing distillation before Christmas. Distillation always has to be careful, 'every plate takes away a petal from the rose' they say, and the speed of heating and cooling also affects quality.

Quite a number of fine winemakers (like their brethren in Burgundy) make grappa almost as a by-product of their wines, and they take good care to ensure that their grappas are worthy of their name. But, increasingly, the best grappas are being made by specialist distillers, often relatively small, who are not distracted by the need to concentrate on their wines. Inevitably, however, given the sheer number of firms and families involved, a lot of what the French call the *artisanale* grappas on the market are rather muddy, heavy and badly made. But there are now dozens which more or less accurately reflect the qualities of the grape variety from which they derive. Varieties such as Brachetto and Nebbiolo and even the aromatic Muscat seem to adapt well to the process, providing rich yet delicate brandies.

ITALIAN BRANDIES

Four provinces compete for attention: Piedmont in north-western Italy, and Friuli, the Veneto and Trentino in the north-east where most of the best specialist distillers are concentrated. Although some of the most respected are in Friuli and the Veneto, the hinterland behind Venice, Trentino, the river valley leading north in Austria, has more small specialists in the finest tradition of Italian industry. Moreover the region has a long tradition of making fine wines and spirits, dating back to the days, less than a century ago, when it was part of the Austro-Hungarian empire. The Trentinese use a special type of still, a *bain-marie* which is often used in other regions. This allows the raw material to be heated indirectly, and relatively gently, by steam, avoiding the bitterness and inequalities of flavour liable to result from sudden, directly applied heat. By contrast in Friuli the *vinaccia*, landing on plates within the still, is in direct contact with the steam. Because the stills in Trentino are so small (holding a mere 600kg of *vinaccia*) most of the resulting spirit can be used, with only a small proportion of the heads – the first spirit which comes off – returned for redistillation and most of the tails – the lower strength last liquid out of the still – can also be used. Most of the spirit emerges at around 70 per cent alcohol, roughly the same as cognac. Legally it can be sold at any strength between 38 and 50 per cent alcohol,

CLASSIC BRANDY

though virtually all the grappas on the market weigh in at 40–43 per cent.

The Trentinese are lucky that the climate in the uplands above the River Adige are relatively cool, so the *vinaccia*, like that from Piedmont, is fresh and sufficiently acidic. Moreover the region now grows so many varieties, both native and international, that the grappa-lover has a wide range to choose from. Fortunately, too, vineyard land in the Trentino is scarce and expensive, so that every drop of juice and shovelful of lees is valuable and worth keeping fresh. In the words of one local: 'we're virtually condemned to make good grappas to justify the cost of the raw material'. The locals, proud of the quality of their product, have already introduced a series of regulations ensuring that the lees are distilled fresh and have now applied for it to be allocated a DOC, the first in Italy for a grappa.

Opposite
The rolling countryside in Friuli which produces Nonino's splendid grappas.

ITALIAN BRANDIES

CLASSIC BRANDY

GRAPPA DIRECTORY

BERTAGNOLLI

This perhaps overly publicised but nevertheless excellent family distillery in the Trentino offers a naturally floral Muscat. They also make an excellent Cabernet Sauvignon, a variety which in other hands can be rather grassy. Fortunately this one is rich and Burgundian with a rather farmyardy nose, sharp, tannic, very long, a classic example of a grappa made from black grapes. Their Traminer is a beautiful grappa with overtones of buttered apples.

BOCCHINO

This is one of the biggest and most innovative of specialist grappa-makers. It has been family-owned since it started distilling as far back as 1898 in Canelli, heart of the Asti Spumante country, south of Turin in Piedmont. The operation is now run by the fourth generation of the family, Carlo and Antonella, the self-styled queen of grappa. The hype –

ITALIAN BRANDIES

which also involves a distillate of orchids – is justified by the fine grappas made from Muscat and Nebbiolo, as well as a prize-winning Barbaresco – achieved by an 18-month stay in French oak which gives it an agreeable nutty flavour. They also make a wood-aged Riserva which could be described as a vatted grappa since it is a blend of Dolcetto, Barbera and Moscato.

BRUNELLO
Based in Vicenza and one of the best grappa-makers in the Veneto, this family business has been distilling since 1840. They select only the best *vinaccia* from local growers and age their grappas for a couple of years to enhance and deepen their varietal characteristics.

CASA GIRELLI
A family firm which is one of the pioneers of single-varietal grappas in the Trentino. As well as an aromatic but slightly heavy Muller-Thurgau, their I Mesi range includes two prize-winners, an excellent Moscato, and a Teroldego, a local grape which produces a rich and fruity grappa.

Below
The patriarchal Giovanni Girelli and his family.

 CLASSIC BRANDY

ITALIAN BRANDIES

MAROLO

One of the best grappa-makers in Piedmont, justifying their high prices, not only by the prettiness of their labels but also the quality of their single-variety grappas, all with delicious, stylish only-in-Italy labels.

CLASSIC BRANDY

MASCHIO MARCELLO

These are excellent grappas from the Veneto. They make dual-variety grappa from Tokay and Merlot which they call Goccia d'Oro and age for seven years in oak. The Cabernet is a ten-year-old.

NARDINI

These were the original makers of grappa in the heartland of the drink's production, Bassano del Grappa in the Veneto. In 1779 their founder, Bartolo Nardini, bought a house at the end of the bridge across the Brenta river, thus attracting

ITALIAN BRANDIES

the passing trade. They used to be purely distillers of unremarkable industrial grappas which have captured a quarter of the Italian market, selling four million bottles annually. But they have now moved upmarket. Their Aquavite di Vinaccia and the Riserva are strong – 50 per cent alcohol – made from a number of varieties and, in the case of the Riserva, aged (for an unknown period) in oak.

NONINO

A family firm in Fruili, founded in 1897, which is one of the pioneers of single-variety grappas (they claim to be the first). They started distilling marc from the local Picolit grape as early as 1973. Since then they have proved to be among the most dynamic propagandists for single-varietal grappas, combining elegant bottles with serious, and seriously individual, brandies often made from little-known local varieties. The family's most astonishing achievement, however, is their UE, their grape brandy made from whole grapes and distilled slowly in traditional stills, then matured in small casks for ten years, resulting in an unusually rich and complex brandy.

Opposite below
The bridge across the Brenta in Bassano del Grappa in the Veneto, birthplace of the spirit named after the town, thanks to the initiative of Bartolo Nardini whose shop stood at the end of the bridge.

CLASSIC BRANDY

PILZER
Small family business in the Trentino where Ivano Pilzer produces delicious grappas from a wide variety of grapes, including Muscat, Chardonnay and Traminer, as well as some local varieties, Nosiola and Schiava. They keep their brandies in stainless steel vats for a few months to give them extra roundness without losing their fruit.

PISONI
Arrigao Pisoni's family supplied the grappas which nourished the participants in the Council of Trent, the series of discussions lasting 30 years which enabled the Catholic Church to formulate its response to the Reformation in the early 16th century. Not surprisingly the family's grappas are pretty classic – and classy – stuff.

GIOVANNI POLI E FIGLI
The Trentino is riddled with members of the Poli family making their own (often excellent) grappas. Giovanni Poli makes some of the best, including a number of rich, oily, little numbers from black grapes and a Muscat which is smooth, oily and not too aggressively characteristic of that grape.

ITALIAN BRANDIES

JACOPO POLI

This is one of the most serious of all specialised grappa producers in the heart of the Veneto. It was founded in 1898 – or at least first officially registered – after some years of bootlegging by Jacopo's grandfather. The stills, which are among the oldest in Italy, are effectively pot-stills operating a batch process, hence the unusual richness of the brandies. They are also complex, made from one or two varieties and some are aged in French oak. They also produce regular brandies aged for at least three years. The family even has its own grappa museum – in Bassano di Grappa, naturally.

Classic Brandy

Rovero

One of the best distillers in Piedmont, and still run by the brothers Rovero. It was founded in 1880 but its real success started in 1920 when one of the family returned from the United States after the start of Prohibition. Today the Roveros mature distinctive grappas, made from a wide range of often obscure local grape varieties, for between two and seven years. Their Barbera has a rich stalky nose and although I found their Dolcetto a little murky, their Freisa has delicious vanilla overtones, the Malvasia a rich plummy

nose, and the Ginestra nice medicinal overtones. But for me the finest and most elegant was the Brachetto with a fine floral nose and a delicious bouquet, reminiscent of dried apricot skins.

VILLA DE VARDA

A distinctively individualist firm in the Trentino which prides itself on its own variant of the *bain-marie* method. Even its choice of grape varieties is unusual, for their 12 single-varietal grappas include a number of local varieties like Marzadro, Livia and Latrari, as well as a superbly rich, long and grapey grappa from the local Marzemino black grape.

BRANDIES FROM AROUND THE WORLD

ARMENIA

Opposite
A monastery in the mountains of Armenia, historically the home of some excellent brandies.

One of the two republics in the Caucasus (the other is Georgia) with a long-established tradition of making wine and a more recent record of making brandies superior to those found elsewhere in the former Soviet Union. Archaeological evidence suggests that vineyards were in existence as far back as the 9th century BC. Greek scholars, including Herodotus and Xenophon, referred to Armenian wines, while, later, monks started to distil aromatic brandies from local, usually sweet, grape varieties. Until recently most of the brandies were consumed within the Soviet Union, often at the drunken banquets which were such a feature of the life of the Soviet *nomenklatura*.

ARARAT

The Ararat distillery in Yerevan, which was bought by the French group Pernod-Ricard in 1998, is responsible for nine-tenths of the country's brandies and has been producing brandies since a major distillery was built in 1887. The quality started to rise after the arrival in 1892 of one Mekertich T Musinyants, who had studied at Montpellier in southern France and introduced what the Armenians call 'the Charentais type of equipment'. By 1901 the Armenians were exporting what they called 'Selected Fine Champagne' brandy. Thanks to Musinyants' heroism, the distillery survived the horrible years of World War I when the Turks massacred over a million Armenians.

Thanks to the 'twelve Charentais machines' – that is pot-stills – the distillery can produce seven million litres of pure brandy every year. Among the firm's more upmarket offerings are Dvin, named after the ancient capital of Armenia, and made from brandies at least ten years old. This was first sold in 1945, in time to be drunk by Winston Churchill and the other statesmen attending the Yalta conference. In 1967 Yerevan introduced another ten-year-old, Akhtamar, named after an island in Lake Van which houses a famous cathedral. Even more upmarket is Tonakan, first produced in 1957 from brandies of over 15 years old. Nairi, named after an old region of Armenia, has an average age of 20

BRANDIES FROM AROUND THE WORLD

years. Kilikia (the name of the ancient Kingdom of Armenia) is the oldest as it is supposedly made of brandies between 20 and 100 years old.

All these brandies are well made and increasingly mellow with age. In the latest list there is, perhaps not surprisingly, no mention of Yerevan, first produced in 1947 to celebrate the 30th anniversary of the Russian Revolution and marketed as the strongest brandy in the world, weighing in at 57 per cent alcohol.

AUSTRALIA

The scrupulous professionalism characteristic of Australian wines also naturally shows through in the brandies offered by the handful of companies, all long-established in the brandy market. They use every type of still: pot-stills – some cylindrical – and column stills, and then mature the brandies for at least two years in oak casks. But the final quality of their two types of brandies, those for sipping and the majority used for mixing, is inevitably limited by the neutrality of the grape varieties used. These are often rather curious varieties such as the Palomino used to produce sherry. Although the distillers are allowed to acidify twice, during fermentation and before the second distillation, the result is not comparable with brandies produced from naturally acid grapes.

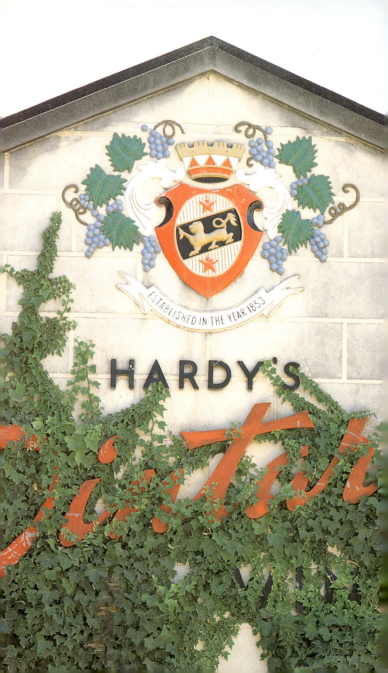

BRANDIES FROM AROUND THE WORLD

In the 1970s the federal government dealt a body blow to the brandy industry by slapping on greatly increased taxes. And although since then the government has tried to make amends by fighting against imports of cheap and heavily subsidised French grape brandy, consumption continues to decrease.

Opposite
By Australian standards, Hardy's is an historic name.

ANGOVE'S

A long-established family-owned wine and brandy concern which, since 1925, has been double-distilling Saint Agnes brandy in pot-stills. They now offer three types, all aged in small oak casks: the XXX, designed as a mixer, the rounded, grapey XXXXX Old Liqueur, which is at least ten years old and the XXXXXXX XO, which is at least 20 years old (a lot more than

Above
Angove clearly sells its brandies by the truckload.

191

CLASSIC BRANDY

most XO cognacs). It's a dark chestnut colour but very elegant and well rounded, and thoroughly deserves the numerous prizes it has been awarded.

BRL HARDY

Major winemaking group which produces a number of excellent brandies. Even the basic three-year-old Black Bottle is half pot-still brandy and offers an apricot colour and a sweet, slightly grassy nose. The seven-year-old Liqueur is fresh and approachable, with the feel of a VSOP cognac and good grapiness. The XO is even more serious with some serious *rancio* and overtones of plain, dark chocolate. Warm, long and fiery on the finish.

McWILLIAMS

McWilliams is one of the top three brandy makers, naturally proud of its own type of continuous still and has been family-owned for over a century. The result is a series of brandies which can be thought of in the same light as distilled old amontillado sherries. The basic Max XXX has a light colour, a good delicate nose but is buttery-rich on the palate, making it an ideal mixing brandy. The XXXX Chairmans Reserve has the same qualities, only more intensely so. However, it's the XXXXX Show Reserve Deluxe Liqueur brandy, currently a blend of the 1963 and 1973 vintages, which is the firm's pride and joy. Distilled three times in a pot-still, it's my favourite Australian brandy, offering length, grapiness and an excellent structure; ending with delightful overtones of almond.

CALIFORNIA

The production of Californian brandy is typically American, divided as it is between very large and very small units. The industrial, or rather industrial-scale, brandies include some – like the former market leader made by Christian Brothers – which use some imported spirit. By far the biggest seller among the purely Californian brandies is that made by E & J Gallo on a vast scale, with sales of over two million cases a year. At the other end of the scale are a handful of small distilleries, often attached to equally minuscule wineries, which are trying to produce what are often rather self-consciously special brandies and grappas. They have a distinctively

Classic Brandy

BRANDIES FROM AROUND THE WORLD

Californian touch, eschewing what they see as the neutral style of old-world spirits and aiming for maximum fruitiness. Some of them have banded together in a body called the 'Artisan Distillers of California'. Tracking them is a problem since they change products (and even owners) with bewildering rapidity. As a result the list is incomplete and does not include many of the experimental grappas now being produced from individual varieties.

Brandy has a long and not especially distinguished history in the USA. Until Prohibition it formed a normal part of the range of most major winemakers in California, along with port and sherry. But it was not generally thought of as a separate, quality product; rather it was a residual product, made from wines which were not good enough to be sold as such. In the 1870s when James Shorb, a typical pioneer, found that many of the million bottles of wine he was making every year proved unsaleable, he reverted to selling only brandy (the same fate

Left
Germain Robin, established by a member of the Robin family from Cognac, operates in a decidedly laid-back style.

195

CLASSIC BRANDY

befell the grapes produced by Governor Leland Stanford at his Vina vineyard). But there were exceptions, like one Henry Nagele, who in the 1860s was making brandy from Riesling and Pinot Noir in the Santa Clara Valley south of San Francisco. He consistently won prizes, especially for the brandy made from Pinot Noir, which he called 'Burgundy brandy'.

After Prohibition had been repealed brandy remained a relatively ordinary product although its commercial importance has grown over the decades. Moreover the shortage of wine grapes ensured that most Californian brandies were (and still are) made from two varieties, Flame Tokay and, above all, the prolific but neutral Thompson Seedless, grown and distilled, not in a winemaking area but in the San Joaquin Valley. Although a few distillers use pot-stills, most California brandies are continuously distilled and then immediately diluted to 50 per cent alcohol before being matured in casks made of American oak, generally ones which have

Right
Jepson's vineyards are as rugged and picturesque as anything in the Trentino.

Brandies from around the World

CLASSIC BRANDY

previously been used to mature bourbon whisky. This experience naturally adds to these brandies' richness.

The making of brandy is well regulated. Only Californian grapes can be used, and the spirit must be distilled to below a maximum of 85 per cent alcohol. The spirit can be flavoured by up to 2.5 per cent of what the Americans confusingly call 'rectifying agents'. These include caramel, liquid sugar, fortified wines, and the juice of prunes and other fruit, fresh as well as dried. The result naturally tends to be brandies made in the Spanish style, although most of them are rather lighter, and are designed to be drunk, not neat, but with a mixer as a 'one-bottle bar', i.e. a spirit that can be drunk with any type of non-alcoholic mixer, thus avoiding the need to have more than one spirit in the house. Typically, the brandy made by the Gallo family is a light, unremarkable spirit made in continuous stills, and marketed specially to be drunk with orange juice. The longest-established brand, Christian Brothers, is a much lighter and more characterful spirit.

But the future of Californian brandy, at the quality end anyway, lies with a handful of brave pioneers who are trying to make a superior product using fine wine grapes and have veered away from the classic notion of using only rather characterless varieties like Ugni Blanc. California always tries to be different, and sometimes, dammit, it succeeds.

BRANDIES FROM AROUND THE WORLD

CHRISTIAN BROTHERS
Still one of the biggest brandy producers, they have a distinctively light style, largely because they use the green-appley Thompson Seedless variety. Their standard brand is clean, light, with a touch of sweetness. Their XO aged Premium Brandy, about half of which is pot-still, is fragrant and oaky.

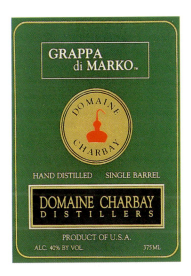

DOMAINE CHARBAY
This family business started distilling in 1983 but is only now releasing its brandies – a true sign of seriousness. The Karakasevic family's varietal pot-still brandy, from an eclectic mix of

CLASSIC BRANDY

Folle Blanche, Pinot Noir and Ugni Blanc, was released at the end of 1999 together with brandies made separately from each of the three varieties. Since 1987 the Karakasevic family has offered the aptly named California Original, described as 'a magical marriage of Chardonnay wine and soft, rich, liqueur brandy'.

E & J GALLO

As one might expect from the Gallo family, owners of the dominant firm in the wine

BRANDIES FROM AROUND THE WORLD

business in the United States, the brandy they introduced in 1968 (called simply E & J) became a best-seller almost immediately. Inevitably, too, it is exceedingly well made and reliable, with a nose of light prune and sweet cherry. If it lacks any real distinction it is still a better mixing product than many other more expensive and pretentious spirits.

CLASSIC BRANDY

GERMAIN-ROBIN ALAMBIC INC

This is a joint venture between Hubert Germain-Robin, a descendant of the Jules Robin family which was once a power in Cognac, and Ansley J Coale Jnr, an Oxford-educated former professor of history. The result is one of the most serious native brandy-making businesses in California. Coale and Germain-Robin specialise in making brandies from a number of grape varieties, black as well as white. Even the single-varietal grappas they make in strictly limited quantities come from a wide range of grapes. Where they are really out of line with virtually all other brandy-makers (except Charbay and RMS) is in using the Burgundian Pinot Noir variety, not only for their XO but also for their other upmarket blends like Shareholders Blend, Old Havana and above all their 16-year-old Anno Domini.

Their single barrel brandies are made from Gamay and Pinot Noir, which, says the firm, make 'extraordinary distilling material, complex, smooth, very fine'. The result is indeed complex and interesting enough to suggest a considerable, and highly individual future for the new-style Californian brandies. Apart from the basic lack of acidity in the grapes, all their rich and complex brandies are among the very few Californian brandies that can be compared with cognac.

Opposite
Germain Robin's distillery is properly orthodox – unlike some of the grape varieties in the stills.

CLASSIC BRANDY

GUILD WINERIES

Producers of several distinct brandies, made from a number of grape varieties including Ugni Blanc and California Tokay, this company mostly continuously distils and then matures their brandies in small American oak casks. Among their offerings are Cresta Blanca, a deliberately heavy and oaky ten-year-old, Ceremony, five years old, dry and only moderately oaky, Cribari, three and a half years old, matured in old casks and therefore light, and Guild, a similar if rather sweeter and oakier brandy.

JEPSON VINEYARDS

Signature Reserve is a high-grade brandy made by Bob and Alice

Right
The aridness of the Mendicino valley is well caught by this photograph of one of Jepson's vineyards.

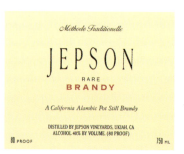

BRANDIES FROM AROUND THE WORLD

CLASSIC BRANDY

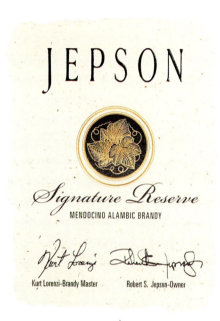

Jepson – both dedicated wine-growers in Mendecino County – from a small plot of the Colombard grapes used in Cognac in the 18th century. Using a traditional pot-still they make a mere 150 cases of brandy a year, aged for five years or more in classic Limousin oak casks. The more widely available, though misleadingly named, Rare Brandy, made from Colombard grapes, has been widely praised by some serious tasters for its fruitiness and complexity.

Brandies from around the World

Korbel

The Korbel family moved from Bohemia to the Russian River north of San Francisco and were growing grapes and making wine and brandy by 1868. In 1954 the firm was sold to the Heck family which has enhanced Korbel's reputation for making fine sparkling wines. The brandy is made in continuous stills to produce a light mixing brandy. But maturation in a Spanish-style *solera* system provides a welcome touch of warmth.

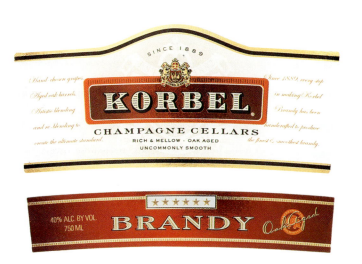

CLASSIC BRANDY

Above

The cognac-style distillery established nearly 20 years ago by the RMS subsidiary of Rémy-Cointreau produces some of California's finest and most original brandies.

RMS

Founded in 1982 by Rémy Martin under the name of RMS and now owned by Piper-Heidsieck, another member of the Rémy-Cointreau Group. From the start RMS refused to compromise and set high standards previously unheard of in California. Nevertheless the distillers were prepared to use techniques developed in Cognac to distil grapes from a number of grape varieties, some of them – such as Pinot Noir – unlikely ones. RMS now produces complex fruity brandies based on six

BRANDIES FROM AROUND THE WORLD

varieties, including what is probably the only Folle Blanche grown in California.

The Quality Extraordinaire 14-Year Rare Alambic Brandy is an excellent product, light, deep and expressive, with a little *rancio* on the nose, comparable to a good brandy from the Fins Bois, though a little young and burny on the finish for its age. The ten-year-old Pinot Noir has a light apricot colour with a nice bitter-orange feel on both nose and palate. A long, lingering, interesting and rather puzzling brandy.

FROM AROUND THE WORLD

CHILE

PISCO

Historically pisco was made in both Peru and Chile. Today the best is obtained from Muscat grapes produced thanks to the unique microclimate of a section of the Elqui Valley in Chile naturally called *Zona Pisquera*; a unique region with narrow valleys of fertile soil surrounded by sunny hills. The climate is warm and dry with sharp contrasts of temperature between day and night and an exceptionally clear atmosphere, ideal conditions for producing Muscat grapes.

Wines were made by the Spanish invaders in the second half of the 16th century and according to Jan Read 'the local availability of large copper vessels and the [Spanish] army's needs in its far-flung operations ensured that grape spirit was probably being made in Chile at least as early as its first manufacture in Holland and France'.

By the end of the 19th century the name pisco was associated with good-quality brandy. In 1931 pisco was granted probably the world's first

Left
The vineyards of the Monte Grande Valley are in a setting bleak enough to create an instant thirst for a Pisco Sour.

211

CLASSIC BRANDY

Opposite
The Mediterranean rockiness of a typical vineyard in Cyprus.

Appellation of Origin ensuring that it could only legally be made in the regions of Atacama and Coquimbo. Today the grapes, mostly grown by small landowners, are harvested between February and May and sold to local co-operatives which use pot-stills. There are two common ways of consuming pisco. The first is as *Piscola*, in which pisco is simply added to Coca-Cola. The second, and by far the best and most popular method is to create a Pisco Sour, which I will describe in a later section of this book (p.250).

CAPEL

The principal company, Capel, produces pisco under its own name, but also produces two other superior quality piscos under the labels of Los Artesanos de Cochiguaz and Alto del Carmen. Pisco comes in a variety of alcohol concentrations ranging from 35 to 50 per cent alcohol.

CYPRUS

Brandy, usually mixed as their own special Brandy Sour, is the country's national drink, a natural by-product of the island's large wine production. Both major distillers produce a special, rather lighter cocktail brandy entirely suitable for their brandy sours.

BRANDIES FROM AROUND THE WORLD

KEO

The Keo group produces a wide variety of wines and fruit juices as well as two brandies: Five Kings is made in pot-stills from the traditional Xynisteri variety, which is used to make the best Commanderias, the island's fabled fortified wine. Five Kings is aged in 500-litre oak barrels for a minimum of 15 years, and thus is smoothness personified. Younger stuff is Commanderia St John.

CLASSIC BRANDY

SODAP

SODAP is best known for its Commanderia but also offers three interesting brandies distilled from the Xynisteri grape. The VO is a young, rather aggressive brandy, the VSOP is lightly woody and delicate, while the upmarket Adonis, which matures for a least 15 years in Limousin oak, is a richer and more satisfying brandy.

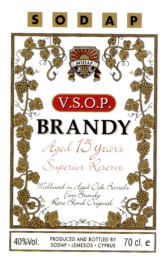

GEORGIA

Georgia, like Armenia, the other brandy-making republic in the Caucasus, has an extremely long tradition of making wine and a more recent record of making brandies superior to those found elsewhere in the former Soviet Union (or in Eastern Europe for that matter). The Georgians, and their brandies and brandy-makers, survived Stalinism well enough since the dictator naturally favoured his native province and its products.

Although the Georgians have been making wine since several thousand years before the birth

BRANDIES FROM AROUND THE WORLD

of Christ, the first 'brandy factory' was established in the capital, Tbilisi, in the 1880s. The founding father was one Dr David Saradjishvili, who had trained in France and Germany. Today virtually all the brandies come from the Eniseli factory, which is now locally, privately owned.

Above
The mountains of Georgia, another great brandy-producer in the Caucasus.

CLASSIC BRANDY

The Georgians use local grape varieties, most of them rather sweet (inevitably in a hot climate), but take great care in distillation and maturation. They use Cognac-type stills, mature the brandies for long periods in small oak casks and even when they have reduced the strength, take care to store them in larger oak casks.

ENISELI

Eniseli markets a range of brandies. The standard offering is three years old. Then comes five-year-old, Dr Saradjishvili, Eniseli (12–14 years), VO (10–21) and Tbilisi (15–20). All are impressive, dry – albeit with a touch of caramel – and mellow. They have plans to sell a 70-year-old and have in stock some 104-year-old though this is only used for blending. But the Georgians are not age-snobs, indeed inside Georgia the Dr Saradjishvili sells for more than the others, largely because it is the only one in modern packaging (in world markets the Georgians are hampered by lack of decent bottles and labels). Eniseli's director, Georgi Chkheidze, prefers the Eniseli, which is made from grapes from eastern Georgia, especially the widely planted Rkatiteli which has high levels of acid and is therefore ideal for brandy production, rather than the Tbilisi, which is made from less acid grapes from all over the republic.

Brandies from around the World

GERMANY

German brandies are relatively anonymous drinks; they have no real heritage, no territorial roots, no real birthplace and no real identity. Indeed, the word used to describe them, *Weinbrand*, was coined as recently as 1907. This is a pity because the relatively acid white grapes that form the basis for German wine production would be highly suitable for making serious brandy. In fact German brandies are simply industrial products, albeit well made ones, perfectly suitable as the base for mixing. They are generally made from semi-fortified wines imported from France or Italy. There are two basic types of German brandy; standard brandies with a minimum of six months ageing and Uralt or Alter aged for at least 12 months. For older brandies the Germans adopt the Cognac designations – VSOP, XO, etc.

ASBACH

It was a young distiller, Hugo Asbach, who in 1907 registered the name Weinbrand. In 1919, after the Germans had been forbidden to use the term cognac to describe their brandies, the word became the generic term for them. Asbach takes

217

BRANDIES FROM AROUND THE WORLD

unusual care in producing its brandies, even though they are mostly made from fortified wines imported from the Charente. These are distilled in Charentais-type stills and matured in French oak in deep underground cellars. Best known is the basic Asbach Uralt – itself a cut above other standard German brandies. Also offered are an eight-year-old VSOP Asbach Privat and the 15-year-old Asbach Selection Extra Old.

Opposite
Asbach's industrial but beautiful distillery is typical of the German approach to brandy.

GUSTAV DECKER

This well-established family company tries harder than most by using cognac-type stills and ageing its brandies for far longer than the competition. Though the nose of the basic Kaiserberg is rather raw and young, it is quite spicy on the palate. The Dupont is less raw but the overwhelming impression is of a generalised toffee-like sweetness. The seven-year-old Steinalter is grapey, slightly medicinal, but fiery on the finish.

ECKES

The biggest brandy producer in Germany with two brandies. Chantre, introduced in 1953, named after the wife of the then chairman, and Mariacron, one of the best-selling brandies in Europe. This was named after a monastery acquired by the family in 1961. Both brandies are continuously distilled – Mariacron, warm and bland, is an excellent mixing brandy.

Overleaf
The decidedly modest original home of Eckes, now the biggest brandy producer in Germany.

 CLASSIC BRANDY

PABST & RICHARZ

Old-established family firm which, as far as I know, makes the only authentic German brandy, since its Pfalzer Weinbrand is made in a pot-still from native grapes.

BRANDIES FROM AROUND THE WORLD

RACKE
This big firm buys wines from the Cognac region and double-distils them in relatively small stills. Its best-selling brandy, Imperial, is bland, caramely, warm, agreeable but unremarkable.

CLASSIC BRANDY

ISRAEL

While Jews have always had a – not always justified – reputation for abstemiousness, there has been a long tradition of Jewish involvement in the alcohol business. The reason was brutally simple; it was one of the few trades permitted to Jews in Eastern Europe, especially those living in Russia. On the excuse that the Jews were responsible for alcoholism among the peasantry, government monopolies were imposed in Russia in the 1880s – encouraging a first wave of emigration to Palestine. Jews were also involved in the alcohol business in North Africa, particularly in Morocco, if only because the Muslim mass of the population was forbidden to have anything to do with alcoholic drinks.

Within Israel the spirits industry really took off between the two world wars and in 1938 Stock, the Italian brandy producer, invested in a distillery, while others were started up immediately after the declaration of independence in 1948. Nevertheless consumption of alcoholic drinks in Israel has always been, and remains,

Right
The Golan Heights, occupied by Israel only since the 1967 war, now produces many of the country's best wines and brandies.

BRANDIES FROM AROUND THE WORLD

CLASSIC BRANDY

lower than that in most developed countries, despite the arrival of hundreds of thousands of Russian Jews who brought with them their native drinking culture. But today new books are being published about alcoholic drinks and there is even a well-attended Israel Bartenders' School.

However, brandy has never been the first spirit of choice in Israel. Immigrants from round the Mediterranean naturally brought with them the taste for anise-flavoured drinks such as arak, while, equally naturally, those from Eastern Europe showed a preference for vodka. Brandy producers also faced the problem of acquiring enough grapes, particularly those with high levels of acid which are the most suitable for brandy distillation. Fortunately today – particularly since the establishment of a winery on the Golan Heights – there is enough Colombard and Chenin Blanc to ensure steady progress in quality; a real requirement since historically Israeli brandy was always regarded, quite rightly, as being far too sweet to be taken seriously by connoisseurs.

BARKAN WINERY & DISTILLERY

From 1938 until 1990 this distillery was owned by the Italian Stock company and a number of their products, like Stock Liqueurs and Julia grappa, are

BRANDIES FROM AROUND THE WORLD

still named after those produced by the previous owners. Indeed the best-selling brandy in Israel is the Stock 84 brandy (outside Israel it is known as King David). This is made from a number of grape varieties continuously distilled and aged for up to four years in large oak casks. The King David Special Reserve is a more serious brandy made from Colombard grapes picked early to preserve the acidity and then single-distilled in a small, 1000-litre alembic.

BARON CELLARS

This represents the most promising quality initiative in the history of Israeli brandy. The Tishbi family had established its first vineyards as early as 1882 but it was only in 1985 that Jonathan Tishbi, the grandson of the original winemaker, called in Sydney Back of Backsberg Winery in South Africa to establish a distillery. In the early 1990s Tishbi bought a Charentais-type pot-still and in 1995 launched the first brandy made in Israel from wines from a single estate, a brandy which is gradually being sold at a more advanced age (originally it was a three-year-old, now it is a four-year-old). It is distilled on its lees following the formula employed by Rémy Martin. When only three years old it won a major prize at a London competition, a tribute to its fruity cleanliness.

CLASSIC BRANDY

CARMEL MIZRACHI

Founded by the Rothschild family in 1882, this remains the biggest winery and distillery in Israel as well as being the biggest exporter of Israeli brandy. The original winery, built in 1890, is the oldest industrial building in use in the country. Distillation, using surplus grapes, started in 1898 and today Carmel produces four brandies, as well as a couple of grappas. One of these – Carmel – is perfectly decent, and all are made with advice from Italian experts.

The four brandies include the three-year-old Brandy 777, the second-biggest brand in Israel, the very good value prize-winning six-year-old Brandy 777 Gold and two luxury products, the nine-year-old Brandy 100 – a prize-winner even though it is rather too sweet for non-Israeli tastes – and another Gold Medal winner, the 15-year-old Brandy 110, sometimes regarded as Israel's leading premium brandy and originally launched 110 years after the first vines were planted round Carmel.

ELIAZ BINYAMINA

This firm, established in 1952, was recently acquired by new owners. But its main product, BBB Brandy, remains the cheapest and naturally least satisfying of all Israeli brandies.

BRANDIES FROM AROUND THE WORLD

SEGAL WINES

Yankel Hirsh Segal built the family's first distillery in White Russia back in 1787. The family emigrated to Israel in 1925 and the seventh generation of the family now runs the winery and distillery (often known as Askalon Wines) in Ramle. The family is a leading importer of wines and spirits and produces a wide range of spirits including two brandies: Grand 41 Brandy – the 41 refers to the brandy's strength – is slightly sweeter than its competitors and thus regarded as the best pre-prandial Israeli brandy and the upmarket, prize-winning Hirshel the Distiller, named after Zvi Hirsch, great-grandfather of the generation now running the business.

MEXICO

The story of Mexican brandy is an extraordinary one. The Mexicans drink over 150 million bottles a year, mostly of Presidente, the world's biggest-selling brand.

Vines were first introduced by Spanish colonists in the early 16th century and today the country makes some well-respected wines, but the real start of the brandy business came just after World War II when the French stopped Mexicans using the term *coñac* so the brand owners adopted the English word brandy. This

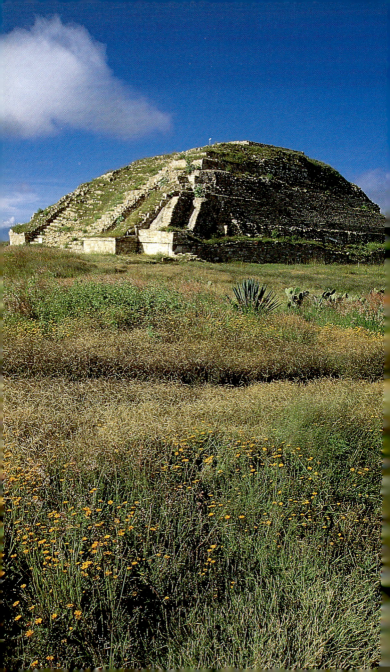

BRANDIES FROM AROUND THE WORLD

change persuaded the Mexicans that brandy, almost invariably mixed with soda or Coca-cola, was an upmarket form of alcohol. Today Mexican brandy sells better than cognac in the United States, and as the Hispanic influence grows, sales are likely to increase.

DOMECQ

The story of Mexican brandy really began in 1947 with the visit of Don Pedro Domecq Gonzalez, head of Domecq, to Mexico. There his local representative Don Antonio Ariza persuaded his chairman to start producing brandy in Mexico. Ten years later Brandy Presidente – named after the country's leader – was launched with an initial sale of a mere 50 cases. Within a couple of decades it was selling millions. It was not only unquestionably the biggest-selling brandy in the world, it was also the only brandy in the world's top 20 spirits brands. Today, although sales have dropped, it is still the biggest-selling imported brandy in the United States.

Like all Domecq's Mexican brandies, Presidente – designed to be light, clean and sweet – is made from the rather characterless Thompson Seedless and Carignan grapes and is continuously distilled. Until 1990 it was aged for three years in a *solera* system in used bourbon barrels (with the charring removed). The age has now been reduced to the six months normal in

Opposite

Monte Alban in Oaxaca, Mexico, a country with an apparently limitless thirst for brandy.

CLASSIC BRANDY

the cheapest Brandies de Jerez, with the natural richness replaced by a woody extract whose ingredients remain a closely guarded secret. Apparently the drop in age has gone unnoticed by drinkers.

In 1964 Domecq (which has been part of the Allied-Domecq Group since 1991) introduced the older, more expensive Don Pedro, now in the world's top 40 spirits (by sales, anyway). Woodier, soft and rich, it contains 10-per-cent of double-distilled brandy and like the Reserva Brandies de Jerez is aged for a year.

In 1974 came the top-of-the-range Azteca d'Oro, named after the Aztecs, the country's most powerful tribe before the arrival of the Spanish Conquistadores in the early 16th century. Dark, clean and sweet, it has 40 per cent double-distilled spirit and, like Gran Reservas, is aged for at least three years.

CASA MADERO

These traditional makers of pot-still brandies have been in business since 1870 when the owner brought a cognac still over from France.

PORTUGAL

In theory Portugal should be ideally placed to produce excellent brandy (*aguardiente*) or marc (*bagaceira*) from the acid white grapes used to

BRANDIES FROM AROUND THE WORLD

make *vinho verde*. But, alas, most of the firms in the business make unremarkable brandies and marcs from a black grape, the Baga – hence, presumably, the description *bagaceira*. However, there are at least three major exceptions.

AVELEDA

This company is a major producer of *vinho verde* and so can exploit its access to sharp white grapes to produce some very decent brandies. Best is the Adega Velha, double-distilled and aged for over ten years in French oak.

Above
Aveleda, as a producer of classic vinho verde, has access to a ready supply of the acid white wine so essential for producing fine brandy.

231

CLASSIC BRANDY

IMPERIO
These dedicated brandy-makers owned by the families who founded the firm back in 1942 produce only an *aguardente*, Vinica Velha Reliqua, using local grape varieties. These are double-distilled and then aged in oak for at least three years to produce a genuinely superior product.

PALACIO DE BREJOEIRA
Maria Herminia D'Oliviera Paes' English is not good but her *bagaceira* is clearly serious since it is made from the lees of the family's *vinho verde* and then aged in small French oak casks for at least seven years.

SOUTH AFRICA

Brandy has a long, and generally disreputable history in South Africa. Today the country is probably the fifth biggest market for brandy in the world and the only major market in which sales are not declining. Brandy accounts for half the market in spirits – Klipdrift Export is the biggest-selling spirit in the country – and South Africa is the only country in the world where brandy is the dominant spirit used in long drinks. This success, however, is largely due to import restrictions during the apartheid period and the steadily depreciating value of the South

BRANDIES FROM AROUND THE WORLD

African rand in recent years, both factors reducing the sale of imported spirits.

Despite its generally high quality (largely due to the unrecognised work done by KWV), within the country brandy retains a relatively poor image – the (almost entirely white) 'brandy and coke' brigade are the country's equivalent of what the British call 'lager louts'. By contrast 'ginger square' – brandy and ginger ale – is the only spirit drunk by respectable white women in the Transvaal.

Brandy was being distilled in South Africa within a few years of the arrival of the first settlers. It was natural for the pioneers, the Dutch, to distil wine, as they had done in Cognac and Jerez. By the end of the 17th century French settlers – many of them Huguenots from La Rochelle on the coast near Cognac – had changed the name of the game. They refused to waste precious wine and started to make pomace brandies from the husks, pips and skins. This resulted in the infamous 'Cape Smoke', also known as *dop* (short for *dopbrandewyn*, or husk brandy) or *witblits* – an Afrikaans word meaning 'white lightning'. This appalling liquid, once described as 'gastric terrorism', had to be distilled at least three times in an – often unsuccessful – attempt to make it palatable. In the early 19th century the British tried to make spirits better than what they called 'Boer Brandy', but the British newcomers, the *Uitlanders* who arrived in

CLASSIC BRANDY

the late 19th century to work the gold and diamond deposits in the Transvaal, were thirsty folk and relied on Cape Smoke which they drank in enormous quantities.

At the turn of the century things started to improve when Sammy Marks, a Lithuanian Jew who was a (improbable) friend of the Boer President Kruger, brought in a Dutch expert, René Santagens, who knew about distillation and maturation as practised in the Charente and when they received backing from a powerful gold magnate, Sir Lionel Phillips. By 1909 the first regulations had been introduced including the encouragement of better brandies through the reduction of duties on 'rebate brandy' which had been matured for at least three years in oak casks. But the collapse of the ostrich feather business in 1914 led to over-production of wine and in the early 1920s brandy production was concentrated in the hands of KWV (Ko-operatiewe Wijnbouwers Vereeniging Beperkt), the Afrikaner-dominated wine and spirits co-operative which slimmed down the brandy business.

After 1945 the Distillers Corporation installed a modern continuous still to produce Oude Meester, a purer spirit eminently suitable to be drunk with Coca-Cola. For its part KWV pioneered what are called Woudberg stills. These are tall cylindrical stills with very tall escape pipes designed for distilling the (usually highly

Opposite
Mons Ruber, typical of the fabulous settings of many South African vineyards.

aromatic) grape varieties used. The KWV distillery at Worcester in the Western Cape, the largest pot-still distillery in the world, contains 120 of them and can handle 3600 hectolitres of wine a day. This helped to supply the market for black South Africans who in 1964 were allowed to buy spirits, and in general prefer better brandies to those bought by white South Africans.

The quality of South African brandies has greatly improved recently. Although most distillers still use a lot of *bonificateur* – corn syrup – over the past 20 years there has been a steady reduction in the use of older additives like rum essence, cloves, cinnamon and synthetic vanilla. In 1987 Distillers introduced the romantically named Flight of the Fish Eagle, the first South African brandy to be distilled purely in pot-stills and during the decade more suitable grapes – like Colombard and Chenin Blanc – became available for distillation where previously distillers had to rely on 'junk' varieties like the oddly named False Pedro. And in 1991 Buks Venter of KWV invited Robert Leauté of Rémy Martin to South Africa to improve the spirits made by the firm, which remains by far the biggest supplier of brandies in the country. Today all the older pot-still-cum-mature grape spirit brands are perfectly decent, but for real quality you have, not surprisingly, to turn to the pure pot-still brandies.

BRANDIES FROM AROUND THE WORLD

THE RULES AND REGULATIONS
There are three types of brandy, all of which have to be matured in oak barrels not exceeding 340 litres in capacity for at least three years:

Pot-still brandy – at least 90 per cent distilled in pot-stills. Must be at least 38 per cent alcohol.

Brandy – at least 30 per cent double-distilled pot-still brandy. Not more than 70 per cent grape spirit. Must be at least 43 per cent alcohol.

Vintage brandy – must be aged for at least eight years, the last five in oak barrels not exceeding 1000 litres capacity. Not more than 70 per cent grape spirit of which at least 60 per cent must be matured for at least eight years in oak casks. Must be at least 38 per cent alcohol.

KWV
Overwhelmingly the biggest brandy distiller in South Africa and one of the biggest in the world. This Afrikaner enterprise has had some difficulty adjusting to the post-apartheid era. But even the sternest critics have to admit that the brandies KWV distils (many of which are marketed by other firms) are all well made and that many are distinguished. Even their basic XXX offers good nuttiness and vanilla overtones, their five-year-old is light in colour and firm on the first nose, but then offers elements of apple and pepper on nose and palate. KWV's ten-year-old is pure pot-still, with a rich grapey nose, a nice nutty feel and good pruny-almondy nougatty overtones on nose and

CLASSIC BRANDY

Above
A typical Cape Dutch doorway in one of KWV's estates.

palate despite a little sweetening from cane sugar. The XO has the feel of well-absorbed vanilla fudge, the 20 years has a nice and, for South Africa, unusual feel of overtones of fruit kernels and dried apricots rather like the Spanish Fundador. In June 1999 KWV introduced – in New York – Imoya, a VSOP brandy described as 'The Spirit of Africa' and clearly aimed at better-heeled Afro-American drinkers. Made from a range of brandies from 5 to 20 years old, all double-distilled, it has a good apricot colour, good warmth and attack, with the backbone of older brandies giving it some depth. But the finest brandy from KWV, and indeed from South Africa, is their Diamond Jubilee brandy, a beautifully balanced spirit with fruity, vanilla and apricot overtones; deservedly one of the very few brandies not from France to have been awarded a silver medal at the International Spirits Challenge.

BACKSBERG

This winery and distillery is run by the third generation of a Jewish family of Lithuanian origins. Michael Back took advantage of a 1990 change in the rules allowing single estate brandies to use surplus Chenin Blanc to make a most promising pot-still brandy.

BRANDIES FROM AROUND THE WORLD

CABRIERE
A fabled vineyard above Franschoek producing superb sparkling wines. The owner, Achil von Arnim, uses his Chardonnay grapes to make a pure pot-still Fine de Jourdan, but to my taste the spirit lacks the bite that would come from a more acid base wine.

OTHER INTERESTING SOUTH AFRICAN BRANDIES
Of the basic brands the best are Bertram's VO (nice feel of liquid fudge, though no relation to the cognac), Martell VO (nice almond-pruny warmth), Oude Meester (rich, pruny feel) and Richelieu Export (light, prunes, nut kernels) – the term Export is misleading since all these spirits contain grape spirit and thus cannot be exported.

Of the better-class blends with some five-year pot-still brandy in them, the best is undoubtedly Kilpdrift Export, which is surprisingly delicate. Of the top-class blends the pioneering Flight of the Fish Eagle remains a star with its delicious light florally lemon nose like a young brandy from the Fins Bois.

And there's one worthwhile oddity: Paarl Rock sells a unique brandy, seven-year-old Haanepot (the Afrikaner word for Muscat), with light and delicate floral overtones thanks to care taken in maturing the brandy and avoiding new oak which would destroy the aromas of the fragile Muscat grape.

CLASSIC BRANDY

THE TASTING OF BRANDY

Even the most experienced wine-tasters often quail at the thought of tasting spirits and it is difficult to blame them, since a proper appreciation depends so much on the nose rather than the palate. Wine-type tasting soon burns up the palate – a process which is greatly speeded up if the brandy involved is relatively young and thus up to 70 per cent alcohol, in the case of cognac. Only a handful of professional tasters can in fact taste more than half a dozen spirits at any one time. The others need frequent breaks, accompanied by copious draughts of water and black coffee, and even then can manage only three flights of five or six samples in a morning. That said, the tasting of spirits can be a most satisfying affair since a fine brandy will have considerable depths to be plumbed, if only because its constituents are so

Chapter Six

complex and so concentrated – distilled in both the popular as well as the technical meaning of the term.

In the past the tasting of brandy was bedevilled by the mystique of the enormous balloon glasses traditionally used. These were a disaster socially because they lent an air of absurdity and snobbery to the drinking of fine brandy and technically because their very size precluded proper appreciation of the aromas. In the words of George Riedel, the glassmaker, 'with large

Below
The nose, rather than the palate, is the brandy taster's most important weapon.

CLASSIC BRANDY

Right
Three classic tasting glasses. (left) George Riedel's glass for the finest brandies – XO and above; (centre) his glass for playing down the harshness inevitable in brandies of VSOP level; and (right) Hennessy's all-purpose glass, its narrow shape designed to concentrate the fumes.

glasses you have large surfaces and lots of evaporation, and this means that the fruit disappears, so all you have left is the alcohol'.

The type of glass you really need is one with a top that is narrower than the bottom of the glass, but, unlike balloons of all sizes, is not too large to allow the flavours to be lost. In my time I've even used a champagne flute, but the best shape is the one used by professional tasters, the bulbous 'tulip glass', which has a small chimney on top of the bulb.

Riedel, ever the perfectionist, now produces not one but three glasses for brandy. None is shaped remotely like a balloon (although, reluctantly, he does have to offer a balloon glass for ignorant traditionalists). His VSOP glass is taller than the usual tulip, and is designed to play up the fruitiness in the brandy and play down the fiery harshness, the burn so evident in even the most reputable VSOP brandies. It works too; a VSOP nosed in this glass is warmer and less fiery than

The Tasting of Brandy

when tasted in the true tulip-shaped glass used for the top brandies. Because these should have lost their youthful harshness, the glass can be designed to maximise the power of the complex aromas of rich chocolatey fruitiness and nuttiness so typical of the finest brandies.

Riedel's third glass is designed for tasting grappa. Tall, thin and elegant the glass 'delivers a very narrow flow onto the tip of the tongue', according to its designer, 'accentuating the fruit and mineral elements of the spirit'. Again Mr Riedel is right, it does help emphasise the floral overtones so precious to grappa-lovers to the forefront of the taste experience.

The appreciation is greater if the brandy is the right temperature. The best is about 18 degrees centigrade, since too warm a brandy evaporates quickly, and thus tastes too alcoholic. Indeed it is not a bad idea to start with a cold brandy and a cold glass, allowing the warmth of the hands to bring the spirit slowly up to the right temperature. If the brandy is already the right temperature it is better to hold the glass by the foot or stem to avoid over-heating.

With brandy, as with wine, the tasting process starts with its colour. But professional brandy drinkers know that this can be deceptive, so the glasses they use are a neutral blue in colour, to prevent appearance from influencing their judgement. For, in theory, the darker and more viscous the spirit, the richer, the 'browner' it will

CLASSIC BRANDY

be, indeed some tasters assume, wrongly, that there is some correlation between depth of colour and the age of the spirit. The widespread use of a chemically neutral colouring liquid by even the most reputable firms is designed to produce a uniform colour. Nevertheless colour can provide a rough guide to a brandy's style – there do not seem to be any dark-brown brandies which taste light and elegant. All the finest brandies, however old, will have a golden streak in their make-up somewhere and they will not be too viscous, too treacly, for this is a sure sign that the brandy has been tampered with.

With brandies, unlike wine, the nosing should be done in two stages to try and separate the more volatile constituents from the heavier ones. So the first nosing should be done without swirling the glass and with the nose slowly approaching the rim of the glass – which can then be rotated slowly rather than swirled – to capture the variety of aromas which should be emanating from the spirit. Then pause to catch your breath and put the nose in the glass to capture the less volatile, more alcoholic components. Only then taste. Now the brandy has to be swirled, just like a wine, to check for the taste components – the fruit, the balance, the length, the finish – which with a brandy will be far longer than with wine. Indeed the aromas of the best brandies will linger for days, lending a magical sweetness to the glass.

Opposite
Holding the glass by the stem avoids warming the brandy too much.

CLASSIC BRANDY

THE MIXING OF BRANDY

Most brandies are designed to be drunk as the basis for long drinks rather than sipped neat, so the trick is to find flavours which blend with brandy rather than fight it. I'm not including one favourite mix, Coca-Cola, because it's so sweet that any taste in the brandy is drowned. In general, of course, the richer the brandy, the more suitable it is to stand up to other strong tastes.

The simplest mix is with ice. As Jacques Denis, a distinguished cognac producer, points out, the cognacs from the Grande Champagne which normally need at least a decade to mature can be drunk young with ice to soften their otherwise aggressive character. Moreover to have some character left after you've popped in the ice you need a brandy somewhat stronger than the standard 40 per cent – by no coincidence his elegant Vieille Reserve is sold at 44 per cent alcohol.

Just as simple is that old stand-by of English clubs and country houses, 'b and s' – brandy mixed with soda, or any other type of relatively neutral fizzy water for that matter. Personally I prefer Perrier as a mixer, finding the slight saltiness an agreeable counterpoint to the richness of the brandy, but other brandy-bores claim that the bubbles in Perrier are rather large and that Badoit is a better mixer.

The other key mixers are ginger ale (which must be dry, like Canada Dry and not the sweeter

The Tasting of Brandy

American Ginger Ale, the brandy is quite sweet enough) and any form of citrus fruit – apart from grapefruit which I've never been tempted to try.

COCKTAILS

There are a dozen basic cocktails involving brandy and below is a small selection of the best known. You can vary the proportions to your own taste and use the sort of glass you fancy but these are the official recipes.

BRANDY ALEXANDER

The beloved drink of Anthony Blanche in *Brideshead Revisited*, although Blanche obviously preferred the alternative recipe which uses heavy cream.

  1oz cream
  2 teaspoons whipped cream
  ¾oz creme de cacao (dark)
  1oz brandy
  nutmeg

Shake well over ice cubes in a shaker, strain into a cocktail glass, sprinkle with nutmeg.

BRANDY SOUR

  2 shots brandy
  1 shot fresh lemon juice
  1/3 shot sugar syrup
  1 shot pasteurised egg white
  4 drops Angostura Bitters

Shake all ingredients, pour into glass and garnish with Opie's cherry.

CLASSIC BRANDY

PIERRE COLLINS

¾–1oz lemon juice
¼–¾oz sugar syrup
2oz cognac
club soda
maraschino cherry
orange slice

Stir first three ingredients well over ice cubes in a collins glass, fill with soda, add the cherry and orange slice.

PISCO SOUR

¾oz lemon juice
¼oz sugar syrup
1½oz pisco brandy
1 dash of bitters
1 egg white
maraschino cherry

Shake well over ice cubes in a shaker, strain into a sour glass, garnish with cherry.

BRANDY FLIP

1 egg yolk
¼oz sugar syrup
¾oz single cream
1¾oz brandy
nutmeg

Shake well over ice cubes in a shaker, strain into a cocktail glass, sprinkle with nutmeg.

BRANDY HIGHBALL

2oz brandy
ginger ale
spiral lemon twist

Pour brandy over ice cubes in a tall glass with ginger ale, add the spiral lemon twist.

MANHATTAN

1½oz brandy
¼oz dry vermouth
¼oz vermouth rosso
1 dash of bitters
maraschino cherry

Stir well in mixing glass, filled with ice cubes, strain into a chilled cocktail glass, garnish with cherry.

BRANDY BLAZER

2 shots brandy
1 cube sugar
1 twist lemon peel
1 twist orange peel

Pour ingredients into 9oz glass. Flambe the mix and stir with a long-handled bar spoon. Extinguish and pour into a clean glass.

GLOSSARY

Aguardente Portuguese term for brandy.

Aguardiente Spanish word for high-proof spirit (70–80 per cent) made in a continuous still.

Airen Rather characterless grape widely planted in Spain and used for Brandy de Jerez.

Alcohol From the Arabic al-kohl, meaning to stain, the powder used to stain eyelids, and thus by extension any kind of fine impalpable powder. Finally, and crucially, the idea of concentration, of the quintessence of the raw material involved.

Aldehydes Chemical compounds halfway between alcohol and organic acids. Formed during maturation and useful in small quantities.

Alembic A pot-still, a term derived from the Arabic word al-ambic.

Alquitara Spanish term for brandy distilled (either once or twice) in a pot-still.

Bagaceira The Portuguese term for marc.

Boisé An additive produced by infusing oak chips in hot water and brandy and used to beef up and age artificially brandies that are too characterless.

Bonbonne A glass jar holding 25 litres used as a neutral container to store brandies once they have sufficiently matured in wood.

Brandewijn (Brandvin, Brandywijn) A Dutch word, literally 'burnt-wine'. It became the international term for the alcohol produced by distilling wine, proof that the Dutch were the pioneers of the commercialisation of alcohol.

Brouillis Spirit of about 30 per cent alcohol produced in the first distillation in a pot-still.

Calandre This unusual system of distillation is used only in the Distillerie Goyard at Ay which buys all the surplus lees from the Champagne region. The wines are first heated by steam in three interconnected vessels each holding about 400 litres. The fumes they give off, which are about 20 per cent alcohol, are then distilled to about 70 per cent.

Chapiteau Literally a circus-tent, 'the Big Top'. In practice describes the small round container which traps the alcoholic vapours emanating from a pot-still.

Col de Cygne Literally 'swan's neck'. This form of ducting between a pot-still and the condenser provides an infinitely smoother path for the brandy than the older, more angular designs.

Colombard Grape variety used in Cognac in the 18th century and in California and Armagnac today.

CLASSIC BRANDY

Congeners A portmanteau term for the many and various impurities found in a spirit, whatever its origin, when it is distilled below 100 per cent alcohol. Obviously the lower the degree to which the raw material is distilled the higher the percentage of these impurities – reaching a maximum of something over 2 per cent of the total in armagnac distilled in the older type of still to barely over 50 per cent alcohol.

But these 'impurities' are precisely the ingredients which provide spirits with their character and thus their interest to the drinker. Hence the need to arrive at a delicate balance to include as many of the aromatic congeners as possible without their noxious brethren. The distiller's task is further complicated because these congeners are so many and varied, including aldehydes, polyphenols and more or less aromatic esters. Up to 150 may be present in a newly distilled spirit, whether it be whisky or brandy. When the brandy is distilled the combination of the spirit with the wood produces up to a further 200 as a result of oxidisation resulting from seepage of air through the wood and by the inter-reaction of the spirit and the chemicals in the wood, most noticeably the lignins and the tannins.

Destilado Spanish term for brandy of over 80 per cent alcohol.

Distillation The concentration of wine (or any other fermented fruit or grain), the separation of the constituents of a liquid mixture by partial vaporisation of the mixture and the separate recovery of the vapour and the residue.

Ethyl alcohol Also known as ethanol, the alcoholic constituent of alcoholic drinks.

Folle Blanche Floral variety of grape making delicious brandies. Little planted now because it is susceptible to rot.

Fine Traditional French term for any type of brandy.

Fusel oils Generic terms for the unpleasant-smelling chemicals that should be removed by distillation.

Gennes Burgundian term for marcs.

Grappa The Italian equivalent of marc, and thus, technically, a pomace brandy.

Heads (*têtes*) The first spirit to flow from a pot-still. Generally discarded or redistilled.

Holandas Measure of strength for Brandies de Jerez, below 70 per cent alcohol.

Phylloxera vastatrix Louse which destroyed virtually all Europe's vineyards in the last quarter of the 19th century.

Pomace brandy Generic term for all

GLOSSARY

types of spirit (marcs, grappas, etc) made from the lees of the grapes.

Rancio A quality developed by brandies, most obviously by cognacs (hence the French term *Rancio Charentais*) when they have been maturing in wood for 20 years or more. Chemically *rancio* derives from the oxidation of the fatty acids in the spirit, producing the ketones which produce the richness felt on the palate with such brandies. This bears no relation to the artificial richness and woodiness imparted by the addition of caramel, or of *boisé* used to provide some artificial age to a brandy.

This richness emerges in a complex series of sensations on the nose and palate. Rankness, a special character of fullness and richness was the unflattering description given by Charles Walter Berry, the wine merchant who was Britain's leading cognac connoisseur between the wars. This richness, allied to a certain mild cheesiness in the nose, reminds some tasters of Roquefort cheese. But to English palates the richness, depth and diversity of *rancio* brings forth memories of the rich fruit cakes traditionally made at Christmas.

Solera The ageing system used in Jerez to mature both brandies and sherries. Oak casks are piled three high and the wine or spirits drawn off the bottom one for bottling at regular intervals, often two or three times a year. The liquid is then replaced from the casks above. This regular decanting both aerates the liquid and speeds up the ageing process.

Tails (*queues*) The end of the run of the spirits through a pot-still. The lower the strength of the final spirit the richer it is in congeners and other aromatic, but sometimes undesirable elements. Brandy-makers wanting a richer final product have to take a chance with the impurities in order to preserve as much aromatic matter as possible.

Tannins Group of chemicals that occur in the bark of many trees, and found in the oak casks used to mature wines and brandies.

Tête de Maure Literally Moor's head, the shape of older-fashioned ducts leading from a still to the condenser. It retained more of the impurities and thus produced a richer, less uniform brandy than the modern *col de cygne*.

Ugni blanc Also known as Trebbiano. Acid, relatively neutral variety of grape almost universally used in Cognac.

Vinaccia The Italian word for the lees of the wine from which grappa is made.

Weinbrand The German word for brandy coined by Hugo Asbach, in 1907.

CLASSIC BRANDY

ACKNOWLEDGEMENTS

Practically everything I have learnt about brandies over the past sixteen years has come from conversations with the people – which in most cases means distillers – who carry with them the many secrets involved in brandy-making and tasting. Among the many let me select just a few to thank: Alain Braastad of Delamain, Bernard Hine, Maurice Fillioux and his nephew Yan of Hennessy, Robert Léaute, formerly of Rémy Martin, Marie-Claude Ségur of the Bureau National Inter-professionel de l'Armagnac and Buks Venter, formerly the presiding genius behind KWV's brandies.

My agent, Robert Ducas, my publisher Barry Winkleman, and his editor Kate Ward, have shown exemplary patience in dealing with an author who considers himself much easier and more malleable than he obviously appears to others.

PICTURE ACKNOWLEDGEMENTS
The Advertising Archives 97; Cephas 39, 55, 119, 192; Hutchison Picture Library 189, 212, 215, 217, 225, 231; Vin Mag Archive 7, 18, 43, 62, 127.

Thanks also to the following for the generous use of their archives:
AE Dor 59; Angove 191; Asbach 220; Bocchino 168, 172; Camus 24–25, 69, 73, 247; Château de Beaulon 22–23, 36; Château de Montiban 33, 107, 114, 122; Courvoisier 78; Eckes 220–221; Frapin 65; Gautier 86; Germain Robin 196, 205; Gonzalez Byass 147; Hennessy 91, 93; Jepson 199, 207; Lustau 137; Martell 20, 45, 49, 52; Nardini 171, 182; Nonino 170, 177; Osborne 150–151; Ragnaud-Sabourin 30, 31, 57, 102; RMS 210–211; Sanchez Romate 137; Sempé 111; Torres 157, 159 and Villa de Varda 161, 167.{\rtf1\ansi \deff4\deflang1033{\fonttbl{\f0\froman\fcharset0\fprq2 Tms 7,

INDEX

additives 33, 57, 58-9
Adex 116
ageing brandy 33-8
  armagnac 108-14, 115
  Brandy de Jerez 138-40, 153
  cognac 53-8, 62-5
  grappa 168
  South African 237
aguardiente 138, 153
Airen grape 137
alcoholic strength 24-5, 28-9, 32
  ageing 35-6
  armagnac 108
  cognac 51
  EEC regulations 38-9
Allied-Domecq group 45, 75, 143, 230
alquitara 153
Alsace 133
Alto del Carmen 212
Angove's 191-2
Ararat 188-9
armagnac 104-31
  ageing 108-14, 115
  alcoholic strength 108
  directory 116-31
  distillation 31, 32, 107-8, 111-13
  regulations 115
Armenian brandy 186-9
Asbach 217-19
Audry 66
Aurian, Philippe 116
Australian brandy 189-93
Aveleda 231

Backsberg 238
Baco grape 116
  22 A 107
Baga grape 231
bain-marie stills 173
Barkan Winery & Distillery 224-5
Baron Cellars 225
Baron de Sigognac 116
base spirit *see* wine spirit
Bertagnolli 176
Bertram 239
Bisquit 56
Bobadilla 141, 142
Bocchino 166-7, 170, 176-7
Bois Communs (Ordinaires) 48, 49
Bollinger 78
Bon Bois 48, 49
Borderies 22-3, 47, 48, 49, 56
Bouju, Daniel 68
Bouron, Louis 69
Boutinet 69-70
Brachetto grape 172
Brandy Alexander 247
Brandy Blazer 248
Brandy de Jerez 134-53
Brandy Flip 248
Brandy Highball 248
Brandy Sour 212, 247
Brillet, Maison 71
BRL Hardy 190, 192
Brunello 177
Burgundian brandy 132-3
Buton 160

Caballero, Luis 142, 146-7
Cabernet Sauvignon grape 176
Cabriere 239
California Tokay grape 204
Californian brandy 193-209
  directory 199-209
  history 195-6
  regulations 198
Camus 22-3, 71-2, 73, 98
Cape Smoke 233-4
Capel 212
caramel 58-9
Carignan grape 229
Carmel Mizarachi 226
Casa Girelli 177
Casa Madero 230
casks 33-6, 53-4, 109-10, 138-40
Castarède 104-5, 116-18
Castel-Sablons 72
Catalan brandy 154-7
Chabanneau 73
Champagnes (region) 42, 46, 48-9, 56-7, 133
Chardonnay grape 182, 200, 239
Château de Beaulon 20-1, 73
Château de Cassaigne 119
Château Laballe 119
Château de Lacaze 120

253

CLASSIC BRANDY

Château de Laubade 120
Château Montifaud 74
Château de Tariquet 120-1
Chenin Blanc grape 224, 236, 238
Chilean brandy 210-12
Christian Brothers 193, 198, 199
Clés des Ducs 122
Coffey stills 24, 26, 31-2
cognac 40-103
  ageing 53-8, 62-5
  directory 66-103
  distillation 24-5, 27, 28, 52-3
  history 40-6
  region 46-51
  regulations 62-5
Colombard grape
  Californian brandy 206
  French brandy 51, 107, 123
  South African brandy 236
colour of brandy 243-4
Compte system of ageing 62-4
congeners 20, 108
continuous stills 24, 26, 31-2, 107-8
Courvoisier 44-5, 75-7
La Croix de Salles 122
Croizet 45, 62, 77
Cyprian brandy 212-14
Daguin, André 122
Darroze, Francis 122-3

Davidoff 77
Decker, Gustav 219
Delamain 54, 78-9
Denis, Jacques 79
destilado de vino 153
distillation 20-32
  armagnac 107-8, 111-13
  Brandy de Jerez 137-8
  Burgundian brandy 132
  cognac 52-3
  grappa 165-8, 170-4
  history 12-17
Distillerie Goyard 133
Distillers Corporation 234, 236, 239
Domaine Charbay 199-200
Domaine de Boingnères 123-4
Domecq 140-1, 142-3, 229-30
Dor, AE 57, 80
Duboigalant 81
duty 15-17

'Early Landed Late Bottled' brandy 64-5
Eckes 219, 220-1
EEC *see* European Economic Community
Eliaz Binyamina 226
Eniseli 215, 216
esters 29
Etablissements Papelorey 127
ethyl alcohols 20, 29

European Economic Community (EEC) 38-9

Ferrand, Pierre 81
Fillioux, Jean 82
Fins Bois 47, 48, 49, 56
Flame Tokay grape 196
Folle Blanche grape 20
  Californian brandy 200, 209
  French brandy 50-1, 107, 121, 123, 127
  Spanish brandy 156
Frapin 54, 82-3
French brandy 40-133
  Alsace 133
  armagnac 104-31
  Burgundy 132-3
  cognac 40-103
Friuli 165, 167, 173, 174-5
fusel alcohols 20, 29-30, 32
Fussigny, A de 83

Gallo, E & J 193, 198, 200-1
Gamay grape 202
Garvey 144
Gascony 104-6, 114
Gautier 84
Gautret, Jules 85
Gelas 124-5
Gemaco group 84
Georgian brandy 214-16
Germain-Robin 194-5, 202-3
Germany 217-21

254

INDEX

Gewürtstraminer grape 133
Godet 86
Gonzalez Byass 141, 144-5
Gourmel, Leopold 87
Gourry de Chadeville 88
Gran Duque d'Alba 141, 146
grape brandy 8
grape marc 8-9, 39, 132-3
grapes 17-20, 51
 see also individual varieties
grappa 9, 39, 163-85, 243
Guild Wineries 204

Hardy, A 88
Hardy, BRL 190, 192
Hennessy, Jas 44, 53, 89-91
Hine 62, 92
holandas 134, 153

Imperio 232
International Spirits Challenge (ISC) 11, 77, 81, 83, 124, 131
Israeli brandy 222-7
Italian spirits 158-85
 brandy 158-62
 grappa 163-85
Janneau 126
Jepson Vineyards 196-7, 204-6
Jerez, Brandy de 134-53
Jura 133

Keo 213
Kilpdrift Export 232, 239
Korbel 207
KWV (Kooperatiewe Wijnbouwers Vereeniging Beperkt) 233, 234-6, 237-8

Laberdolive 126-7
Larresingle 127
Larsen 93
Latari grape 185
lees 8-9, 39, 132, 165, 170-2
Lheraud 93
lignins 36, 38
Livia grape 185
Los Artesanos de Cochiguaz 212
Lustau, Emilio 137, 146-7
LVMH Moet Hennessy 89

McWilliams 192-3
De Maillac 127
making brandy 12-39
 ageing 33-8
 distillation 12-17, 20-32
 EEC regulations 38-9
 raw material 17-20
marc 8-9, 39, 132-3
Marolo 179
Marquis de Montesquiou 128
Martell 44-7, 54, 89, 94-6, 239
Marzadro grape 185

Marzemino grape 185
Mascaro 154-6
Maschio Marcello 180
maturation *see* ageing brandy
Merlot grape 180
Mexican brandy 227-30
mixing brandy 246-7
Moet & Chandon 89
De Montal 128
Moyet 96
Muscat grape 172, 176-7, 182, 211, 239

Nardini 169, 180-1
Nebbiolo grape 172, 177
Noah grape 107
Noblige 96
Nonino 167, 168, 181
Normandin-Mercier 96-8
nosing 244
Nosiola grape 182

oak
 casks 33-6, 53-4
 chips 33, 57, 59
Osborne 142, 147-9
Otard 98

Paarl Rock 239
Pabst & Richarz 220
Pacabeo grape 154
Palacio de Brejoeira 232
Palomino grape 189
Parellada grape 154, 156
Pernod-Ricard 128, 188
Phylloxera vastatrix 110, 134
Picolit grape 181

255

CLASSIC BRANDY

Pierre Collins 248
Pilzer 182
Pinot Noir grape 196, 200, 202, 208, 209
Piper-Heidsieck 208
pisco 211-12
Pisco Sour 212, 248
Piscola 212
Pisoni 182
Planat 98
Poli e Figli 182
Poli, Jacopo 183
pomace 8-9, 39
 see also grappa; marc
Portuguese brandy 230-2
pot-stills 20-1, 24, 26-30, 52, 111-12
Presidente 227, 229
Prince de Didonne 99
Provence 133

Racke 221
Ragnaud, Raymond 99
Ragnaud-Sabourin 54-5, 99-101
rancio 57-8, 59
regulations
 armagnac 115
 Brandy de Jerez 153
 Californian brandy 198
 cognac 62-5
 EEC 38-9
 South African brandy 237
Rémy Martin 44, 53, 54, 101-3, 208
Rémy-Cointreau 122
Richelieu Export 239

Riesling grape 196
Rkatiteli grape 216
RMS 208-9
Roullet 103
Rovero 184-5
Royer, Louis 16, 103
Ryst-Dupeyron 128

Saint Emilion grape *see* Ugni Blanc grape
Samalens 129-30
Sanchez Romate 135, 140, 141, 149-50
Schiava grape 182
Seagram 45, 94
Seagram-Martell 126
Segal Wines 227
Sempé 109, 130-1
SODAP 214
solera system 138-40
South African brandy 232-9
Spanish brandy 134-57
stills
 bain-marie 173
 continuous 24, 26, 31-2, 107-8
 pot-stills 20-1, 24, 26-30, 52, 111-12
 Woudberg 234-6
Stock 161-2, 222, 224-5
sugar syrup 58-9
Suntory 103

tannins 36-8
tasting brandy 240-8
tax 15-17
Terry 151
Thompson Seedless grape 196, 199, 229
Tiffon 103
Tokay grape 180
Torres 155, 156-7
Traminer grape 182
Trebbiano grape 160
 see also Ugni Blanc
Trentino 159, 165, 173-4

Ugni Blanc grape
 see also Trebbiano
 Californian brandy 200, 204
 French brandy 20, 52, 107, 123
Unicognac 103
United States brandy 193-209

Valdespino 151-2
Veneto 173, 180
Villa de Varda 164, 185
VSOP brandy 64, 242-3

Weinbrand 217-21
wine spirit 17-19, 20-32, 38
 Californian 198
 French 51-2, 108
 Italian 173-4
 Spanish 137-8
wood chips 33, 57, 59
Woudberg stills 234-6

XO brandy 64
Xynisteri grape 214